Small Happiness
& Other Epiphanies

Small Happiness

& Other Epiphanies

SPARROW

MONKFISH BOOK PUBLISHING COMPANY

RHINEBECK, NEW YORK

Portions of this book first appeared in the essay "Small Happiness," published in the July 2015 issue of *The Sun* magazine.

Fireflyy and Max Powow are fictional musical artists invented by the author.

Paperback ISBN 978-1-948626-29-3
eBook ISBN 978-1-948626-30-9

Library of Congress Cataloging-in-Publication Data

Names: Sparrow (American poet), author.
Title: Small happiness & other epiphanies / Sparrow.
Other titles: Small happiness and other epiphanies
Description: Rhinebeck, New York : Monkfish Book Publishing Company, [2020]
Identifiers: LCCN 2020030908 (print) | LCCN 2020030909 (ebook) | ISBN
   9781948626293 (paperback) | ISBN 9781948626309 (ebook)
Subjects: LCSH: Happiness. | Conduct of life.
Classification: LCC BJ1481 .S6594 2020 (print) | LCC BJ1481 (ebook) | DDC
   170/.44--dc23
LC record available at https://lccn.loc.gov/2020030908
LC ebook record available at https://lccn.loc.gov/2020030909

Book and cover design by Colin Rolfe
Cover and interior illustrations by Sparrow

Monkfish Book Publishing Company
22 East Market Street, Suite 304
Rhinebeck, New York 12572
(845) 876-4861
monkfishpublishing.com

To Dadaji Daneshananda, my spiritual advisor

Contents

Introduction

I was visiting my friend Srinivas in Chandannagar, India, when his father entered the room. The elderly man held a stick of incense, rang a bell, and chanted Sanskrit in a low murmur while hovering over some small statues on the dresser. "My father is a Brahman," Srinivas explained, a little embarrassed. "He goes around blessing the deities several times a day."

I was envious; I wished *my* father had such devotional rituals, rather than just reading the *New York Times* and watching Turner Classic Movies.

Most of the readers of this book are not deeply religious Hindus, I imagine. How can we, as citizens of the USA, practice daily domestic blessings? Should we walk through our homes three times a day kissing our eggbeaters and ironing boards? Perhaps. This book is full of such modest suggestions for beautifying the "aura" of one's household.

When my daughter Sylvia was twenty-two, I felt the urge to pass on my wisdom to her—so I had to quickly invent some eternal truths. This became "Small Happiness." Later I wrote the sequel, "Smaller Happiness," which was logically smaller than the original.

Young people seek ecstasy, and they find it. But those dramatic highs have a way of evaporating, leaving one querulously forlorn. The smaller the happiness, the more durable, I have learned. I wanted Sylvia to know this.

"Eat Your Dreams" is a true story (though I'm not certain I actually lost weight). In fact, nearly everything in this manuscript is true. The gods blessed me with few desires, a subsistence wage, an extremely patient wife, and manifold eccentricities—resulting in the life history you are about to timorously encounter.

I write this in the midst of the world lockdown caused by the coronavirus. For writers, quarantine is eternal. They sit in soundproof rooms as far from their husbands as possible, forgetting to brush their hair and wash their clothes. Inside their minds is the witch goddess Lamarzia or their stern fourth-grade teacher. I am a member of this tribe. At the moment, millions of new members have inadvertently joined our coterie. Welcome!

My advice: start small with small happiness. The first day, fill up your life with pointless distractions: YouTube, Facebook, reruns of *Family Guy*. But put aside three and a half minutes to cultivate small happiness. The second day, lengthen that period to three and five-eighths minutes. Each day, increase your dose of contentment minutely. Eventually, small happiness will permeate your existence. You may even reach mid-sized happiness.

Actually, I don't care whether you follow my suggestions or not. I have not yet registered the Sparrow Foundation of

Small Happiness (such a moment may be approaching). Feel free to ignore my unwieldy theses. Write your own book, or encyclopedia, of minimal pleasures—and don't even mention me in the acknowledgments!

Sparrow
Phoenicia, N.Y.

PART 1

Small Happiness

Happiness starts small; learn to recognize it. It's like a weed we see every day but cannot identify.

Small happiness is generous. If you win $12 million, you'll hide it from your friends, but if you're given a free pizza, you'll share it with everyone.

If you want big happiness, take ayahuasca. If you want small happiness, wake up early. At 6:00 a.m., the world hasn't had time to generate trouble. The birds tentatively sing. The sun tentatively brightens the sky. The day starts small.

Big happiness is visual; small happiness is aural. We've become a culture so attached to moving images that we've forgotten how to hear. We never turn off all the lights, close our eyes, and listen to Debussy. All music has become background music. New music is even written for that purpose! But listening is a key to small happiness.

Sex researchers have discovered that many women believe they are "frigid" because they don't recognize their own orgasms. They expect the convulsive ecstasy of a porn video. Their orgasms seem too small.

Now consider: Ninety-nine percent of the orgasms in porn movies are faked. Therefore, many women (at least of the ones who watch porn movies) are missing their true orgasms because they've been brainwashed by false orgasms. In the same way, we all pursue the illusion of ecstasy, missing the small moments of happiness that appear and reappear in our lives.

Medicine created the concept of the "false negative," a test which incorrectly comes back negative. For example, a test may show that you don't have COVID-19 when you actually do. But one may have a "false negative" of the Soul as well. You may believe your life is tragic, pointless, wasted, but your "test" may be inaccurate. Beware of the philosophical false negative!

You can't force happiness, great or small, but you may invite it. One way is to slow down your life—literally. Walk through your house like you're walking through olive oil. If you always use a dishwasher, wash your dishes by hand. If you already wash them by hand, take ten minutes longer. Don't try to get the dishes cleaner, try to get them slower.

Turn off the TV in the middle of a show and stare at the wall. Try to learn what the wall is telling you.

Many of us "fight depression" rather than seek happiness. One of our goals should be to discover new amusements—to multiply our joys. Seek out something you love that you never knew you loved.

Improve your handwriting. Spend ten minutes a day for a week, attempting to make your penmanship more lovely.

Last night I sat on the sofa during a thunderstorm, flossing my teeth. Every minute or two lightning would flash—quite close—and I could see, through the glass door in the kitchen, the backyard flare up brilliantly. The bushes and trees were as bright as in afternoon but lit with a madman's light: cold and white. It was like watching a horror movie without characters.

To achieve happiness, your life must have a purpose. I'm sorry, but this is true. How do you find a purpose in life? Here's one way: take a simple fifteen-minute walk and see if the universe offers you guidance. Quite likely this whole concept is nonsensical—the universe doesn't "offer guidance." But try it anyway. What have you got to lose? Fifteen minutes?

Choose a one-day hobby! True, most hobbies last for years, but just for once, take up a hobby for a single day. Play the harp; collage maps; climb smokestacks—the choice is up to you. But pour all your passion into a twenty-four-hour spree!

The kindest (and cheapest) gift is a handwritten letter. (In fact, if you want to save fifty-five cents, you may slip it under your friend's door.)

Go outside and listen to rain. If you live on the twelfth floor of a thirty-eight-story building, walk downstairs and stand under an awning. Humans were intended to hear this contrapuntal pattering. Listening to rain massages the psyche.

We all search for happiness, but we rarely succeed in locating it. Much better is to sit completely still and let happiness search for you.

Small pleasures are often pleasures of repose. Sit in a corner of your bedroom and listen to the silence. Corner silence is more profound than mid-room silence.

Happiness is basically the same as health. When you're healthy, you feel mighty. When you are ill or feeble, you're irritable. The New Age has ruined the word "healing," and anyway, I prefer "convalescing." Begin your convalescence!

My advice is to loosen your expectations. Most people say, "Lower your expectations"—which is also good advice, but not *as* good. Let me give a concrete example why. Let's say you're going to Cape Cod for five days. You expect your vacation to be perfect: five days of bright, summery weather. To your astonishment, two of the days are rainy; one is absolutely gloomy. Only two of the days are what you expected. Your vacation is a "failure."

So the next time you visit Cape Cod, lower your expectations.

Instead of perfect weather, expect five days of pure hell. Plan
for the waiters to curse you, lightning bolts to strike your cottage, thieves to steal your car. When, in fact, you experience
three rainy days and two nice ones, you'll be overjoyed.

But I'll go even further. I say to you, on your next trip to
Cape Cod, *loosen* your expectations. This time, have no fixed
ideas; expect neither joy nor misery. Notice how life feels
without a future.

Small happiness is always a surprise. It can't be created. Your
best bet is to encourage serendipity. That's one reason I play
a musical instrument three minutes a day, though I have no
musical talent. Usually six of my notes will surprise me.

We are told by television and the Internet what will make
us happy—but they're wrong. One mistake we all make is
searching for other people's happiness. Each person's happiness is different. You know you're finding your own particular
joy when it strikes other people as weird.

The fastest way to small happiness is through love. And it
doesn't matter whom or what you love—snails, your grandma,
Sweden. Even celebrities! Lately I've been watching videos of
Blondie, the New Wave band, from 1979. Yes, I'm in love with
Debbie Harry! But it hurts no one, not even Debbie Harry!

Give yourself excuses to love. For two minutes on a Thursday,
send out love to your mailman—even if he's not there! Or love
everyone who's ever been a cashier at Walmart.

A revolution happens when enough women and men love.

Love others from behind. As you walk down the street, direct your gaze at the pedestrians in front of you. Send your dearest adoration to them. Mentally kiss their backs.

The purpose of art is to make us happy. Great art, like the songs of Robert Johnson and the plays of William Shakespeare, gives us a sober happiness, mixed with sadness. Lesser art just makes us smile—or want to dance. Use both types of art in your pursuit of small happiness.

Plus, art teaches us to perceive our world's beauties. This morning I took out a container of cooked soybeans from the freezer, and placed it on the deck behind my house to thaw in the July sun. Twenty minutes later, passing the soybeans, I noticed that they resembled an abstract painting from 1962—the repeated, beige oval shapes trapped in ice. Thanks to my hours in art galleries, I'd discovered a "masterpiece in plastic."

Yesterday I took the Trailways bus from New York City to Phoenicia and found a seat with a small video screen above it. (The screen was blank.) We had a break at Kingston, and as I stood up, I hit my head on the screen—and then I laughed. I enjoy ridiculing my own blunders. My life is essentially a slapstick comedy for an audience of one.

Another small happiness of mine is writing really dumb poems which strike me as funny; here's one:

Misspelled Poem

I am
hopping
to see
you again.

Composing bad poetry helps me appreciate great poetry. The older I get, the more delight I receive reading the Masters. Yesterday, I was astounded by:

John Anderson, My Jo

John Anderson, my jo, John,
    When we were first acquent,
Your locks were like the raven,
    Your bonie brow was brent;
But now your brow is beld, John,
    Your locks are like the snaw,
But blessings on your frosty pow,
    John Anderson, my jo!

John Anderson, my jo, John,
    We clamb the hill thegither,
And mony a cantie day, John,
    We've had wi' ane anither:
Now we maun totter down, John,
    And hand in hand we'll go,
And sleep thegither at the foot,
    John Anderson, my jo!

[That's by Robert Burns.]

In the last two years I've begun to enjoy classical music, partly influenced by my daughter. This is one reason God gives us children: to improve our aesthetics. Sylvia began to listen to Brahms's symphonies at the age of fifteen, and while I was proud of her, I was also mystified. I've always found this type of music pompous, undanceable, with rigid white-man rhythms. But now I can hear the exotic whimsy in Grieg's Piano Concerto for Piano and Orchestra in A Minor, Op. 16, to which I'm currently listening. I will go into my wife's study and listen to Grieg for just two or three minutes, and walk back to my life feeling satisfied.

Two or three minutes of Grieg is a kind of haiku symphony.

Be your own Spotify app! (This used to be called "singing to oneself.") It's more entertaining than just listening. To begin with, you may customize the song—sing "Get Off of My Cloud" by the Rolling Stones with a Japanese accent, or as if you're drowning. You'll have the pleasure of moving your lips and mouth, and perhaps believing for one moment that you are a better singer than Mick Jagger (which is quite possible). No one seems to sing outside the shower anymore—but that shouldn't stop *you*!

There is a Sufi proverb: "Boredom is the gateway to Paradise." (All right, I invented this proverb. But it's true! Or, at the very least, small happiness often emerges from idleness.)

Small happiness feels protective, as if the Good Witch of Oz has cast a spell on you preventing evil from entering a sphere around you. Happiness is safety.

One mostly unexplored pleasure is walking backwards. The same room you've entered forty-three thousand times is suddenly mysterious—and dangerous—when you enter ass-first!

For one thing, you learn to feel with your heels.

In my first year at Cornell I took Philosophy 101 and read George Berkeley. I was astonished to discover, at the age of eighteen, that we cannot prove the world is real. When you turn around, there is no way to establish logically that anything behind you still exists. (Finally, in exasperation, Bishop Berkeley declared that all matter is "ideas in the mind of God.") When you walk backwards, you are plunging into that unprovable unknown. It's an act of faith. Begin slowly!

Lately I've had a word in my mind from the play Abraham Lincoln was watching when he was shot, *Our American Cousin*. In fact, it's the line that came just before his assassination:

> "Well, I guess I know enough to turn you inside out, old gal—you sockdologizing old man-trap."

"Sockdologizing" has been echoing in my head like a song. What a remarkable example of nineteenth-century slang! One small happiness comes from loving words.

Take a cigarette break without the cigarette. Go outside and breathe. (If it helps, you may construct a small paper tube resembling a cigarette to breathe through.) Raise and lower your hand. Look around. Take five minutes, which is the average time for smoking a cigarette, according to Yahoo Answers.

Today at the Phoenicia Market (my dreary local grocery store) the garlic was sprouting. Green shoots curled from the white cloves—a bright, vital green. The garlic resembled a Kandinsky painting.

I love the tininess of life.

Go for a walk. When you see a NO TRESPASSING sign, walk past it, onto private property. Taste the thrill of violating the law.

Within you is a "happiness voice" that you have never noticed. At every moment, this voice is telling you how to feel joyous. (Often it just wants to look out the window.) Learn to heed your "happiness voice."

It is much better to be old than young. When you observe young people, you notice how stupid they are—what foolish decisions they make. (You made the same decisions when you were young; in fact, you made even worse ones!) As you grow older, you grow wiser, without even trying.

Sit for a few moments and notice yourself aging. Feel wisdom entering you.

Happiness must expand. Find a new source of delight you've never found before. Learn to appreciate the music of Siberian shamans, or the smell of spearmint oil. Spend time at your desk designing the perfect pillow.

Sartre wrote, "Hell is other people," and he was right. But the opposite, "Heaven is other people," is also true. One fast route to happiness is playing pointless games—for example, Scrabble—with friends.

Small happiness has no ideology. It isn't Marxist, Free Market, Christian. It exists in a generous world of unity. All happy people are one momentary nation.

Small happiness is forgiveness. If you notice carefully, during moments of happiness you forgive every person who's ever wronged you.

The secret of life is to be manic and depressive at once.

I have loved composting since I first learned of its existence in 1975. The fact that you can take scraps of potato and cabbage, mix them with horse manure and grass cuttings, and create your own bountiful soil is astonishing. It's like cooking in reverse.

Now that composting is officially sanctioned in New York City, I often bring my leftovers—corn husks, parts of a tomato growing fungus—down to the special composting receptacles in my parents' basement. The satisfaction of composting is one of the most valid human happinesses.

In America we all feel guilty for wasting time. This is one way we refuse to be happy. Everyone should repeat this affirmation: "I will waste more time today. I will be unproductive. I will become more and more like a birch tree."

Most of us are too shy to love. We are shy even in front of inanimate objects, like a fence or a Picasso painting. We are too embarrassed to stand around for all to see, staring at a lovely fence. Thus, we miss out on much satisfaction.

Every day, we are punished for shyness.

Once, while staying at my parents' apartment in Brooklyn, I awoke on a Saturday morning to hear a coin being spun on the floor above. Some three-year-old kid was spinning a quarter—or a washer—and watching it slowly fall to the floor, over and over again.

How do I know it's a child, I thought. Because no adult would spin a quarter. How sad!

Here's your next assignment: Visit a three-year-old child. Watch everything that she (or he) does. If you like, take notes. Then go home and repeat what you have learned, but in your own way, merging your twenty-seven-year-old self (or sixty-two-year-old self) with the kid's antics.

The world distracts us from happiness. We even forget to inquire inwardly if we're happy, unless we meet some distant friend or stranger who asks, "How's it going?" And even then, there's only a flicker of a moment before we compulsively reply, "Can't complain." We move through life with happiness amnesia.

I discovered chicory while hitchhiking cross-country in the 1970s. It's a spindly weed with bright blue flowers that grows by the side of the road. I'd be standing on the entrance ramp to a highway in Colorado next to a stand of chicory, and a sympathetic hippie would pick me up, share a joint with me, drive me forty-seven miles, and I'd leave the car, stoned—only to stand next to another chicory plant! I began to feel that this blue-flagged being was a guardian angel of hitchhikers—a flower at once extremely common and supernally lovely.

Now that I live in the mountains, I see chicory daily through much of the year. Sometimes it's as low as a dandelion, sometimes as tall as a fourteen-year-old. The flowers are bizarrely tenacious. They start in July and persist as the oak leaves die around them. No empty lot, no dirt road is too humble for chicory, with its cerulean blue just like the Virgin Mary's robe.

Memory can be a source of small happiness. This morning I awoke visualizing the stamp collection I had when I was ten. How I loved that album, filled with solemn Danish prime ministers and French *fleur-de-lis*!

Happiness expands time. Thirty seconds of delight seems longer than an overcast afternoon.

Happiness requires protection. You must learn to build a wall
around your small happiness. Shield yourself from the outer
world, with its daily tragic headlines and public fears. Small
happiness also requires privacy. (Later you may lower your
wall and catch up on the latest disaster.)

Speaking of small happiness is almost indecent. It's like taking
photographs of a naked woman through a keyhole. The small
pleasures of life should remain private. The only reason I vio-
late their sanctity is to help you, my reader.

A new bumper sticker:

HEAVEN HAPPENS

For moments, we break free of Earth and enter eternal
Paradise.

PART 2

Smaller Happiness

Sometimes, when I visit my parents in Brooklyn, I do my meditation on one of the benches across the street from their house. One day, as I was meditating, I heard two men passing. One said: "The best way to learn is slow."

L'Allegro, Il Penseroso, Comus and Lycidas by John Milton is one book I am studying slowly. Last night, while flossing my teeth, I read:

> The spirit of Plato, to unfold
> What worlds, or what vast regions hold
> The immortal mind that hath forsook
> Her mansion in this fleshly nook:
> And of those dæmons that are found
> In fire, air, flood, or under ground,
> Whose power hath a true consent
> With planet, or with element.

This small part of *Il Penseroso* stirs the stilled heart—even if you can't understand what it means!

A man named Ken Booth is running for the local town council (as a Republican) so he sent me a free wooden ruler attached to a campaign flyer. Now I can measure exactly how small my happiness is! My guitar pick, for example, is 1 3/16 inch by 1 inch. The label on my grapefruit is 1 1/16 inch by 7/8 inch.

I have become a connoisseur of toothpaste. My current favorite is Dr. Bronner's Cinnamon All-One Toothpaste. It tastes like expensive Hungarian pastry.

Crickets are trained musicians, just like those of the London Symphony Orchestra. (Crickets study with other crickets, just like the cellists at Juilliard.)

A few strands of a mop peek out from under the door of my utility closet, looking like youthful gray snakes.

There's a stream that appears and disappears behind my house, depending on the recent rainfall. Today it's thin but fast, making a sound like *goppagloppagoppagloppagoppa*.

Some jars are much more well-shaped than others. In my refrigerator, the best jar is the one holding Cento Capers: it's narrow, elegant, built like a Florentine tower.

An economical rain is falling—rainfall without excess.

Every nursing home has one or two virgins.

I have a "study," a small room in which I'm sitting at the moment, writing on my computer. Last night I brought a guitar into my study and leaned it against the bookshelf. This morning, as I came here, I noticed how a guitar changes a room—the mellow dignity it radiates. (It happens that this is an utterly out-of-tune, seven-string guitar that Violet, my wife, bought in Russia in 1971.)

I mentioned to Violet that I love the new Ellsworth Kelly postage stamps, so she kindly bought me a sheet of them. Do you know his art? It's very minimal: large canvases with bright colors, usually one color to a canvas. Kelly, who died in 2015, mixed his colors himself and spread them with inhuman evenness. His paintings are the happiest of any great artist. (An article on the Artnet website is entitled: "Are These New Ellsworth Kelly Stamps the Most Beautiful Stamps Ever? Yes, They Are.") When I place a Kelly stamp on an envelope, I feel like an artist myself.

We are constantly being instructed, during this quarantine, to wash our hands. Luckily, I enjoy lathering my palms—not just washing them, but working up a significant lather. Do you? My wife buys "natural" soaps, which don't produce many suds, so I got a cake of Ivory from the food pantry, and now I produce a substantial cloud of white soapiness. Balancing mounds of suds is a bit like sculpting clay.

I lived in Gainesville, Florida, in the 1970s. One day, in 1978, an Iranian guy picked me up hitchhiking and told me: "There will be a revolution in Iran." Six months later, the revolution came. The CIA was shocked, but I knew, because I hitchhike.

Yesterday my friend Ron Rybacki came to visit. "I can only stay a moment; I just came to give you a glassful of popcorn," Ron explained. I brought out a glass, and he poured me twelve or fifteen popcorn puffs from his Smartfood bag.

Later, my wife ate the popcorn.

I have a blue cloth cap which has slowly become so stretched that it resembles fifteenth-century Flemish headgear—specifically, the "chaperon." It's nice to be five centuries out of fashion.

At ninety-nine years old, my father asked his best friend Sam to bring him a good cigar, and now he has a few puffs on the cigar two or three evenings a week, as he sips his Johnny Walker Black. Dad hadn't smoked a cigar in thirty-five years, but suddenly he had a yen for this calming pleasure. At ninety-nine, why not?

I called my dentist's office, and the secretary put me on hold—but there was no repetitive, maddening synthesizer music, just silence. So I walked outside and gazed into the purring stream while I waited.

Today I stood in the woods behind my house and saw a mystifying sight: a brown leaf was attached to the trunk of a sapling by a fragment of spiderweb. A wind made the leaf flutter, but never pulled it off its perch. The leaf was like a kite, attached by the tiniest of filaments.

PART 3

Seasonal Happiness

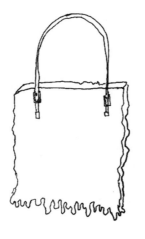

What to Buy for Summer

No doubt your first question when summer arrives is: "What should I buy?" Luckily, this essay will resolve that vexing dilemma.

1) You obviously need a brim hat. And that hat should have a funny slogan on it. The one I'm currently wearing says: "Catastrophe Team" beneath the red umbrella logo of Travelers Insurance. This cap is a cautious beige, allowing the bright umbrella—embroidered in red thread—to stand out like a fire in a bamboo plantation.

2) Also, you really need a pair of sunglasses. Try to find ones that don't strain your eyes or make you resemble a sinister Finnish embezzler.

3) A harmonica is an absolute necessity of summer. Even if you have no musical talent, buy one! Only this instrument conveys the cruel vastness of the lonely post-Hegelian soul. Hearing a mouth harp—originally invented in Germany in 1821—you feel an aching nostalgia for a semi-imaginary cowboy kingdom that you glimpsed at age seven on a flickering TV screen.

4) Other musical instruments are also a good idea. Even if you can't play them, leave them lying around for your semi-nomadic friend Jeff to pick up while he's visiting, so he can regale you with "The Catapult Waltz"! Live music is better for the human body than B vitamins, studies have shown.

5) Get a hose. Hoses are quite useful in summer: for cleaning horsefly corpses off your Datsun, for watering the garden, and, if you have a five-year-old girl, for holding the hose while she dances in the stream of water. (Occasionally you must place your thumb over the hose's nozzle, to spray her.) For some reason, this is the most fun a kid can have.

6) You'll need a bathing suit because, let's face it, you can't always go skinny dipping. One warning: Don't buy a see-through suit, unless you possess the type of body people enjoy beholding. I have yellow polyester bathing trunks which are highly revealing of my anatomy when wet, and I've learned that no one wants to imagine me with a penis.

7) A kite is very useful in the summer. Incidentally, kites have made enormous technical progress in the last seventeen years. For example, there's the wind-harness glider, perfect for raising your pet mouse aloft in complete safety.

8) Send postcards! What is more postally delightful than a cheery rectangle bearing an image of Cape Cod or Gibraltar? Even the most generic postcard message feels personal in this age of ceaseless electronic chatter. For example:

Dear Maurice:

Greetings from The Ensign. Room service in this dump is highly uncertain. I asked them to send up two towels, and three hours later, received a dying onion.

Miss you,
Horace

9) In my youth, summer was notable for its cuisine. The staples of my diet—meatloaf, bologna sandwiches, joyless carrot sticks—were suddenly enlivened with cantaloupe, fresh corn, cherries. And besides that, Gil the Good Humor Man would drive up offering ice cream sandwiches and strawberry pops. So splurge on some toothsome summer treats! One of my long-term goals: becoming an expert on the ripening of plums.

10) Men, buy a razor and shave off your beard! There's no reason to look like a lumberjack at a swinging beach party. Conversely, women shouldn't shave their legs in summer. Thigh-hair is pleasantly vine-like in this lush season.

11) Read comic books! They are the perfect literary form for the season. The trick of summer superhero-reading is to learn which movies will be showing at the Cineplex. Even if you don't actually see them, you'll feel more *au courant* reading the companion comics. (You can tell your friends: "*X-Men: Apocalypse* didn't live up to the print version.") Summer comics should be epic, cosmic, but also jocular, sexy, thrilling, disorienting. Preferably, mutants should mutate *further*, into double-mutants.

12) Now is the perfect time to tape a poster to your wall. In winter, a poster looks saturnine and lifeless, but in summer, a poster sparkles. But whose picture should you choose? I suggest a poster featuring a lyric by Henry Wadsworth Longfellow:

> O summer day beside the joyous sea!
> O summer day so wonderful and white,
> So full of gladness and so full of pain!
> Forever and forever shalt thou be
> To some the gravestone of a dead delight,
> To some the landmark of a new domain.

13) Add a touch of *estival* glamor to your wardrobe! ["Estival" is the adjectival word for summer.] Purchase a small accessory that electrifies your minimal post-Memorial Day costume: a purse made from candle wax, or an anklet with the colors of the Taiwanese flag. (You can sell this adornment at a yard sale on Labor Day!)

14) And a T-shirt! Recently I was walking on Delancey Street in Manhattan when a twenty-six-year-old woman passed me in a T-shirt with the message: CATSKILLS vs. HAMPTONS. I laughed out loud, right there on the sidewalk. (Of course, she didn't even notice.)

15) Summer calls for cool, bracing drinks. If you're a Muslim-style alcohol abstainer like myself, try:

Sparrow's August Refreshment

4 ripe strawberries
1 tablespoon fireweed honey
5 raisins (soaked)
3 drops lemon juice
2 cups organic pear juice

Soak five raisins for two hours, while refrigerating pear juice. Blend ingredients together and serve.

16) This is no ordinary summer, but our quadrennial electoral spasm. Make sure to budget some of your money to support your favorite neo-fascist or dogged feminist icon. I can't tell you whom to vote for, but be generous; our media-savvy candidates desperately need your PayPal account.

17) Buy a silly board game! What is more fun than sitting with two friends on your porch playing Bunny Bunny Moose Moose? (That's an actual game, in which players dress up like bunnies and moose to avoid being shot by a hunter.)

18) Buy large, dangerous fireworks, but don't actually detonate them yourself; hire a fireworks consultant.

19) Buy the song of the summer! Believe it or not, each summer still has a theme song that articulates the mood of the nation. True, this song is mostly known by fourteen-year-olds in Nebraska, but you can own it too! Just Google "song of the summer," see what comes up, and download it, or purchase it as a CD single. (Yes, there are still CD singles!) Last summer (2019) the song was "Truth Hurts" by Lizzo.

Keeping Cool in Summer Is a Breeze!

☀ ☀ ☀

Though it's been a chilly spring—snow is predicted for tomorrow as I write this—summer is approaching, and with it the danger of hot weather. You wonder: How can I effectively cool down my house? Relax. Answers are beginning to flow into my cranium.

Cold-blooded animals can be wonderfully soothing on a humid day. My recommendation: Send your dogs, cats, and hamsters to a friend in the Southern hemisphere—where it's winter—and purchase an Anaconda, iguana, or gecko. An ectothermic creature (the scientific term for "cold-blooded") wrapped around your bare chest is worth two air-conditioners, in my book.

Speaking of books, the right literature can decrease the temperature of an oppressive afternoon. For example, Leo Tolstoy's "Master and Man":

> As soon as they had passed the blacksmith's hut,
> the last in the village, they realized that the wind
> was much stronger than they had thought. The

road could hardly be seen. The tracks left by the sledge-runners were immediately covered by snow and the road was only distinguished by the fact that it was higher than the rest of the ground. There was a swirl of snow over the fields and the line where sky and earth met could not be seen...

Evaporation is a cooling process. Did you learn that in eighth grade? I did. And you know what it means? Get wet, and you'll soon be cool. A Southern remedy for heat is a moist, light-colored towel hung in a window. The evaporating water chills the inflowing air.

Or sleep outdoors! My wife sleeps on our deck on certain sultry nights. (I'm too "citified" to do so.)

Or let the night cool your day! Open the windows at night, close them in the morning, to retain the cool air—then lower the shades of the windows at the south side of the house during the day to prevent your rooms from reheating.

Try to attract mosquitoes. These flying annoyances will take your mind off the heat.

Ice is one obvious answer to summer heat. Ice sculpture is a versatile, underappreciated art form. We all know about ice swans, but did you realize that praying mantises, pickup trucks, hairbrushes, sycamore trees, razor blades, Batman, armchairs, Buddhas, and jewelry may also be constructed from frozen water?

When I lived in Gainesville, Florida, in the 1970s, I would sometimes visit my friend David Hyduke. "Would you like to see my new ice sculpture?" he'd ask. Then he'd open his freezer, push aside the chicken livers and frozen corn, and pull out an abstract shape he'd produced with a blowtorch. We would gaze at it for a while, then David would return the piece to the storage shelf before it melted. Sculpting in ice is always poignant, but in Florida it's twice as touching.

I suggest you order a large block of ice, sculpt it into a life-size statue of someone you admire—Katherine Hepburn, Frederick Douglass, Paul Klee, etc.—place it in the bathtub and occasionally remove your clothes, jump in, and embrace your hero.

Or save a snowball from winter (in one corner of your freezer) and bring it out on the hottest day of July. Wearing a pair of shorts, place the sphere of snow on your knee, and chant:

> Snowball, snowball,
> on my knee –
> I warm you;
> you cool me!

Watch your heirloom snow-orb slowly melt.

Diet can affect internal temperature. Coolness-inducing foods include bananas, yogurt, cucumbers, parsley, asparagus, watermelon, rutabaga, squash, pasta, and azuki beans. Begin preparing and eating them, and notice how your heat-suffering diminishes.

My research partner Eli Tapuchi had this suggestion:

> Turn up the heat, all the way, to 96 degrees! Or past that, if your thermostat will allow it. Keep it that way for an hour, then shut it off. See how much cooler you feel now! (It's similar to what the Bedouins do

to deal with the desert heat: they drink hot tea. It makes them sweat and cools them down.)

Speaking of tea, try Sparrow's Ayurvedic Chillout Punch, composed of herbs that have a cooling effect according to the traditional Indian system of healing. Here's the recipe:

 1 teaspoon spearmint
 1 teaspoon fennel seed
 1 teaspoon fresh cilantro
 1 teaspoon cardamom

 Boil a half gallon of water. Place herbs inside. Once the tea has steeped, cool it in the refrigerator. Serve to discontented, overheated friends.

While you and your pals drink my Ayurvedic beverage, watch terrifying movies! When they give you the shivers, you'll forget it's summer. (I recommend *Q: The Winged Serpent* and *Two Thousand Maniacs!*)

Handheld fans were invented in the Far East. The first European fans were imported from China and Japan, and reserved for European royalty. The montures (sticks and holders) of these air-paddles were made of mother-of-pearl, ivory, and tortoiseshell, sometimes inlaid with gold and silver piqué work. In the seventeenth century, feather fans were the style. Eighteenth century fashion favored silk and parchment specimens—plus the introduction of mechanical, wind-up fans. The nineteenth century brought more democratic fanning technology, made of bamboo, straw, celluloid, starched lace, corduroy, paper, even candy.

My suggestion: Hire four servants to fan you. As an exotic touch, dress them as fourth-century BCE Egyptian laborers: bare chested, with a short wraparound skirt—known as a *shendyt*—belted at the waist. (That's for men.)

But if you're low on money or socialistically inclined, start a fanning collective. Find a group of friends and sympathizers who'll take turns visiting each other's houses and waving fans. Fanning collectives were popular in Costa Rica in the 1920s, until banana plantation owners brutally suppressed them. But don't let that stop you this summer!

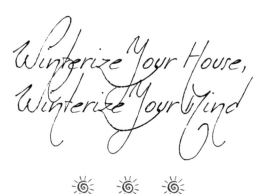

Winterize Your House, Winterize Your Mind

※ ※ ※

When winter approaches (assuming you live in a severe northern climate, as I do), you must prepare your wardrobe, your furnace, your insulation—but also your mind. Numerous experts can help with the first three areas, but I am highly equipped to handle the fourth. Follow these easy steps for mental winter preparation:

Start drying herbs in the summer to drink as tea in the winter. Try mullein and peppermint leaves, chicory and burdock root.

If you have pets, now's the time to flatter and bribe them. You'll want their warm bodies next to you on the mattress nightly from around Halloween until Easter. If you're single and have no bed companion, this might be a good time to flatter and cajole a human being, as well.

Everything you procrastinate over during the rest of the year may be easily accomplished in winter. Why not get political? Call your elected representatives. If you're a liberal, beg them to do something generous. If you're a conservative, ask them to do something traditional. And if you're a Situationist, demand a heroically absurd gesture (for example, insist that Senator Charles Schumer ride into the Capitol building on a rhinoceros).

Pull out all your stained T-shirts with frayed collars. During the summer months, you must wear attractive black T-shirts decorated with snarling red dragons (this describes the shirt I'm wearing right now, which my wife purchased in Wales). In winter months, you can wear the world's crappiest undershirt, because it will be covered by a snug turtleneck.

It is the birdlessness of winter that most disheartens me—perhaps because I myself am a bird, at least in name. Here is one solution to cold-weather despondency: study the songs of autumn birds. (You may do this by clambering through the bosky forest, or by looking up "Northeastern Birdsong" on YouTube.) Learn these calls and sing them to yourself in the January silence. Also, study the ravings of crows, whose strident calls remain when all our other fine feathered friends have deserted us.

Check your floor and wooden furniture for splinters. It's amusing to remove a splinter in August but agonizing to do so deep in February.

Winter is the perfect time to light candles. The days are dim, the nights barren. Consider scented candles. Did you know that wax tapers now exist that smell like Kentucky Fried Chicken and New York City pizza? I'm not making this up.

One traditional winter pastime is whittling. Your local forests can provide the soft wood that's best for beginners: fir, cedar, spruce, pine. Use a pocketknife or a special whittling blade and spend a restful evening producing a tiny sailboat. The next day, paint it! Those of you with more contemporary tastes may wish to whittle Styrofoam into images of iPhones, DVDs, earbuds. Now that's bona fide twenty-first-century folk art!

Wait for UFOs. Flying saucers often appear on a new moon between 1:00 and 2:00 a.m. Also, they may respond to psychic messages—so close your eyes and summon them!

Prepare your musical playlist for the frigid months. Here's where most music-consumers make a big mistake. They listen to frenzied dance music in the summer, delicate string quartets in the winter. Just the opposite would be wise. The cool music of Erik Satie "air conditions" a sweaty August day, while the polyrhythmic sounds of R3HAB inspire dancing in the winter, which warms the body and flexes flaccid hibernal muscles.

It's also useful to have an escape fantasy. Mine is to live in a hut on the edge of the sea in Sri Lanka. (I just looked on a map, and chose Trincomalee, on the eastern coast, as my precise location.) My hut will be bright purple, with a thatched roof of palm fronds and a handy twelve-foot hammock. Vividly picturing my beach cabin makes the infinite glassiness of January more bearable.

Last night, in a dream, I saw a winter coat—inside a boutique—composed of six layers of shirts, vests, jackets, all sewn together. It looked like the garb of a homeless person, only clean and stylish. If I were more entrepreneurial, I'd begin manufacturing them, but instead I'm passing the idea on to you—for free!

Find a pen pal. I'm not kidding! I have a couple of friends I write to on actual paper, and this coming season is the perfect one to cultivate such empathic Victorian pastimes.

I recently published an essay which included this passage:

> We speak of our marriages, our careers, our sex lives,
> but never of our history as readers: our "book lives."
> Reading is just as essential as marrying or being a
> dentist, but we avoid mentioning it. The next time
> you see a friend, ask her, "How's your book life?"

Now, people sometimes inquire about my book life. Well,
I'll tell you one thing. My book life changes in winter.

In the summer, I can gaily read a juicy treatise like *Children
of the Matrix: How an Interdimensional Race Has Controlled the
World for Thousands of Years—and Still Does* by David Icke, but
if I open such a book after November, I'll sense a person in
a gabardine coat standing behind me brandishing a revolver
in a reptilian claw. One of my worst novel-choosing mistakes
was reading the dispiriting *Ethan Frome* during one of my
first Phoenician winters. My advice: Spend your wintry nights
reading happy books set in Bolivia.

When I first moved to the Catskills of 1998, people told
me, "You'll need a winter sport." After years, I finally found
one: Zen Buddhism. There is a delightfully authentic monas-
tery in Mount Tremper, just two miles from my home. You can
go there on a Sunday or Wednesday—for free—and sit in a
chair (or cross-legged). Then you meditate. Here's the method:
As you breathe in, you count "one." Then you breathe out,
and count "two." Your next inbreath is three. Your next out-
breath is four. You continue till you reach ten, then start over.
Meanwhile your eyes are half-lowered—not exactly open, not
quite closed. You do this counting over and over, and an invisible key in your mind turns. (In a sense, Zen really *is* a sport,

because between meditations you do extremely slow walking, which is a fine training in torso balancing.) Meditation is the only winter sport that actually improves one's karma!

PART 4

Practical Happiness

A Guide to Rural Living

❀ ❀ ❀

My wife said to me last night: "I was just awoken by the wind." I lived in Manhattan thirty-five years, and no wind ever woke me up. If you relocate to the hinterlands, you'll be amazed that moving air can sound like a three-hundred-foot-high battleship crashing into a mountain. In fact, there are many surprises here in the Catskills. If you're considering inhabiting a rural enclave, read these instructions carefully—perhaps even twice!

For one thing, bring a sweater. The whole climatological system next to a forest is like a massive air conditioner. I sleep under two blankets, two quilts, a heavy green curtain, a thick bedspread, plus an unzipped sleeping bag—and that's in August!

You will never be disturbed by upstairs or downstairs neighbors, because you won't have any. The closest humans will be about fifty feet away, and will be perfectly benign, except for playing a little heavy metal music on a Saturday night—and even that you won't hear from your bedroom.

Also, time is different here. Out in Western civilization, everyone complains that they "have no time." Here, time is embarrassingly profuse. A typical Tuesday evening is as interminable as your brother-in-law's slideshow of his visit to Portugal. Here in Phoenicia, we have too much water and too much time—especially in winter, when the hours stretch endlessly in all directions, like the ice-covered immensities of Antarctica. I suggest you stock your garage (or attic) with piles of books: Latin American history, rock 'n' roll biographies, feminist mystery novels, opera librettos. And not just books—CDs, cassette tapes, DVDs too. You'll need mucho ammunition in the war against snowed-in boredom.

Also, visual art is different in these parts. What Lower Manhattan calls "art" means nothing up here, and vice versa. A person who can paint a landscape with a red barn that nicely captures the afternoon light is considered an artist in Woodstock; down in Chelsea, such people are as irrelevant as ostriches. Similarly, the latest neoconceptual art installation executed in Brooklyn looks like a pile of trash to an Ulster County watercolorist.

Even if you aren't a menstruating woman, you will develop a very close relationship with the moon while living up here in the Catskills. Three nights out of the month, the moon is unimaginably lustrous—so bright it casts a shadow. On the other hand, for three nights out of the month the night is completely dark; you can get lost in your own backyard.

Warning: trees may begin speaking to you. It happened to me after six years here. Nowadays, a tree in my backyard offers me advice almost daily. I asked her if she wished to speak for this book, and she said (to all of you): "Do everything slowfully."

You will go years without seeing an airplane overhead, though occasionally a black helicopter will fly agonizingly low over your valley, which will plunge you into twenty minutes of anxiety about the CIA. Which reminds me—all of your new friends will be conspiracy theorists, and you'll "learn" a lot about the Federal Reserve. Remember, whenever anyone says, "I'm doing a lot of research on the Internet," it means they're losing their mind.

Upstate radio is quite odd. During the day in Phoenicia, only one station comes in clearly: K104.7, hit radio for teenagers, from Poughkeepsie. At night, however, tantalizing, unpredictable frequencies from distant cities suddenly appear: French news from Montréal; Cleveland Indians baseball; 1930s radio serials rebroadcast from Hamilton, Ontario; WWVA from Wheeling, West Virginia (now entirely Christian); Chinese voices. Often the stations appear, flourish, and dissolve into static within minutes. It's like hearing new outtakes from the Beatles's "Revolution No. 9" every night!

The good news is there are no cockroaches upstate; the bad news is there are mice. You're up against a long and arduous battle with rodents, unless you give up completely or adopt a cat. Each night you must scrupulously sponge the stove; otherwise you'll awaken to tiny cigar-shaped turds beside your burners. My wife and I have evolved past "have-a-heart" traps, because we'd compassionately carry the trapped mice outside, release them, and watch them sneak back in the kitchen. So we began buying old-fashioned murderous traps—but our long-tailed enemies grew smarter and stopped getting caught. (Still, they manage to eat the peanut butter bait. By setting mousetraps, we're *feeding* the mice!) As those who have followed American history in the last forty years know, it's very difficult to win against a disciplined guerrilla army.

In the city, one sometimes sees a celebrity; in the mountains, one occasionally meets a bear. Bears have essentially the same digestive system we do, which means they eat exactly the way you would if you'd never read a book on nutrition. Their preferred diet is pizza, chicken nuggets, Snickers bars—and every day they go dumpster-diving in Phoenicia, searching for these delicacies.

This has been a big bear season for me. My friend Mack and I went walking in Phoenicia Park one day, as a "teenage" bear cavorted nearby. He stood on his hind legs, reaching up to a tree; he lay on the ground; he paced about. At one point, as we sat on a bench, he walked right toward us, either through aggression or myopia. We didn't flinch, and he drifted off to the right. A bear is a fine companion on a Wednesday afternoon.

New York City gets impressive sunsets, due to the thickly toxic atmosphere of New Jersey, but here in the Catskills, a mountain stands between oneself and the setting sun, so all you see are vaguely pink patches above. But at night, the stars are close—even closer than the ones on the ceiling of Grand Central Station. And dawn is exhilarant, with its chill air and voluminous dew. It's like the birth of the world.

So, move to the woods! (But if possible, do it slowfully.)

Some Secrets of Home Maintenance

-ᕧ- -ᕧ- -ᕧ-

My relationship to home repair is like a Manhattanite's concept of cooking: my main task is to dial the phone. (In fact, I am a Manhattanite by birth and grew up in a housing project, where all maintenance was speedily accomplished by city employees.) One of the numbers I dial is Paraco, our propane company, once a year, to ask for a furnace inspection. A gentle but methodical fellow named Ralph comes, cleans our furnace, and saves us from death by frostbite.

Another of my efforts is mice prevention. I wash the dishes every night, then scrupulously wipe the stovetop. Finally, I remove all the trapped vegetable matter from the sink strainer. When we lived in the East Village, Violet and I ultimately shared our apartment with sixty-three thousand cockroaches, due to certain lapses in sanitation. To repent for our sins of the '90s, I am perfectly vigilant today.

Despite my personal inadequacies in home maintenance, I have compiled a list of suggestions for you, precious reader:

1) Name your house. The English do this, and it's always

appealing. Violet and I stayed in a mansion called Colimace in Cheltenham in 1986. Four American soldiers had been billeted there during World War II, and the house's name was a combination of their states of origin.

Here's a suggestion: title your domicile after your favorite beer. "Budweiser Manor" or "Dos Equis Hall" are memorable destinations.

2) Write an anthem for your house. Here is one, based on the Swedish National Anthem:

> Thou ancient, thou free, thou mountain-encircled home;
> Thou quiet, thou joyful and fair!
> I greet thee, most beauteous house upon Earth;
> The noble sun rises above thee!

Sing it every morning when you awaken, just after urinating.

3) Act swiftly. A small problem will grow more grievous. A little leak will get larger. Two mice will become fourteen. I hate to spend money, but I force myself to call the plumber before the bathroom is underwater.

4) Read books on home improvement. At my mother-in-law's house I found the Black & Decker *Complete Guide to Home Masonry.* I quote from Step 14 of "How to Build Garden Steps Using Timbers & Concrete": "Smooth (screed) the concrete by dragging a 2 x 4 across the top of the frame."

Did you know "screed" could be a verb? This alone is a reason to immerse yourself in home maintenance.

5) Dancing improves a room. Aesthetic motion makes a home happier. Late at night while I do the dishes, I listen to K104.7, the station of "today's hit music" out of Poughkeepsie. If I like a song, I'll set down a soapy bowl and undulate around the kitchen. I know my house approves. (At the moment, my preferred song is Tones and I's "Dance Monkey.")

6) Open your windows! I live in a valley full of lively air. Let the air disinfect your carpets and chairs. (Even in winter, open the window two inches for half an hour in the morning.) Two thousand and six hundred years ago, the Chinese philosopher Lao Tzu wrote:

> Cut out windows and doors
> In the house as you build;
> But the use of the house
> Will depend on the space
> In the walls that is void.

Mr. Tzu meant that one should have as much air in a house as possible, and as few objects. Clutter in a house attracts dust, dust attracts mold, mold attracts illness. Material possessions make you sick, in other words—while a chill breeze increases healthiness.

7) Employ the sun! Drape your blankets and towels out on the deck, or on the clothesline. Let the sun cleanse your cloth.

8) Declutter the garage. Here I've learned an important lesson. If you suggest to your spouse, "Let's look around the garage and decide what we don't need," she'll reply, "I can't deal with that right now; I'm overwhelmed." But if you find a particularly

useless-looking item—say, a half-deflated basketball—and ask, "May I throw this out?" she'll answer, "Whatever…"

9) Wash the bathtub. My wife and I bought an elegant clawfoot bathtub—for $100—from a surreal, four-story, secondhand store called Zaborski Emporium. Here's my secret formula for cleaning it: Mix equal parts Arm & Hammer Super Washing Soda and Borax Detergent Booster, add water and smear this paste on the porcelain late at night. Next day, wash it off with a sponge. You need not strain or rub. With no effort, your tub will be radiantly clean! (I have no idea if this works on plastic.) I learned all this from my friend Anique.

10) Don't vacuum. Usually it's unnecessary to sweep or vacuum your house. Just wait for the dust to form "dust bunnies" or "dust mice" (lovely phrases!) and toss them out the front door.

11) Use a plunger! The toilet plunger has existed since the 1860s, and all our space-age digital technology has failed to improve it. (This device also works on stopped-up sinks— though you'd be wise to wash the plunger in a solution of water and bleach first.) Plunging a toilet is a wrenching, vaguely sexual experience. Pushing the wooden handle, I feel heroic, like a medieval knight in a poem by Sir Walter Scott:

> O young Lochinvar is come out of the west,
> Through all the wide Border his plunger's the best…

Of course, occasionally plunging fails, and the results are unspeakably disgusting. But this is true of most projects— even fiction writing.

12) Don't worry. Don't waste time worrying about your house. Houses dislike anxiety. They prefer action, but also enjoy leisure. Either fix the problem, or lie around ignoring it. But worrying makes every crack grow larger.

Compost!

The English language doesn't have a word for a person who expertly composts, though this art is as essential as baking. No one ever says: "Nelly is an ace composter."

A heap of decaying vegetative matter returns one to the pre-digital "real" world. Gazing barefoot at your compost pile, you might be living in the third century BCE. (According to my extensive research, composting began at least with the Akkadian Empire, circa 2200 BCE.) Incidentally, I suggest a 1:2 proportion of food scraps to dead leaves. And don't forget, you can compost paper—including this book!

Then there's the visual aspect of compost. Are you familiar with the outdoor art installations of Andy Goldsworthy? One is a circle of flame-red leaves laid around a jet-black rock, "painting" a Surrealist scene by skillfully manipulating flora. Consider Goldsworthy each time you throw a handful of carrot tops on your compost pile. Let the orange circles offset the pale green broccoli stems and brown leaves to form a pleasing bio-geometric composition.

Composting is part of the great cycle of life: from soil to rutabaga, back to soil. And someday you will step onto this cycle, to become future soil yourself.

Want to combat global warming? Start a compost pile. Food scraps in landfill produce methane, which is twenty-six times more potent than carbon dioxide as a greenhouse gas. Compost produces zero methane.

A compost pile is sensuous, sultry, even sexual. In fact, you might consider having sex with your partner atop a composting heap—to mingle your human secretions with those of rancid parsnips.

How to Be a Singer-Songwriter

Anyone can be a singer-songwriter. It's quite easy. Just think of the last thing you said—for example, "We really need to buy lettuce." Then sing it. If you made up a tune, you are a singer-songwriter. If you borrowed a tune, you're also a singer-songwriter, because putting new words to old tunes is a perfectly valid form of musical creation.

Sing your song again. Now you can add words to it, perhaps about salad dressing, or cucumbers.

Your song may strike you as inconsequential, but others may love it. For every new song there is a fan somewhere.

Your next step is to go to an open mike, and sing your song. You might wish to rehearse it once or twice—but don't over-prepare. Borrow a guitar from a friend, or buy one. Wear the guitar around your neck. Put your name on the list for the open mike. When it's your turn, walk up to the front with the guitar around your neck. Sing your song, but don't play the guitar. Everyone will assume that you will use the guitar for the next song. After you finish your song, stop, smile, and wait for the applause. If your song is short enough, everyone will love it.

Return to your seat. Calculate how well you were received,

on a scale of zero to ten. Decide what you could have done better—whether to make eye contact with the audience, for example. Whether to lean slightly forward or slightly back. Pete Seeger flung his head backwards, as if in ecstasy. The so-called "shoegazer" bands stare at the ground. Which approach is best for you? Possibly alternating the head-fling and the shoegaze.

Now translate your song into a new language—for example, Serbo-Croatian. Ask a friend who speaks that language to help you pronounce it correctly—or if you have no such friends, go on YouTube and watch Serbo-Croatian videos. At your next open mike, stand up and say: "This is a Serbo-Croatian song called 'Shakhleb,' which means 'Lettuce.'" Then sing the song. Afterwards, read the translation. At that point, everyone will either laugh hysterically or look puzzled. Sit down.

It's time to write your second song. Let's make this one a little more profound. Open a book at random and copy down a sentence. For example, I just opened Charles Darwin's *The Expression of the Emotions in Man and Animal*, and came to this line:

> Instead of walking upright, the body sinks downwards or even crouches, and is thrown into flexuous movements; his tail instead of being held stiff and upright, is lowered and wagged from side to side; his hair instantly becomes smooth; his ears are depressed and drawn backwards, but not closely to the head; and his lips hang loosely.

This is the description of a dog recognizing his master. (In fact, that could be the title of your song: "A Dog Recognizes

His Master.") You might want to change a word or two. If you sing that sentence, perhaps in a high trill, even if you are completely out of tune, many people will be impressed. After all, you're singing some of the greatest prose in the English language. This is what is known as an "art song." Franz Schubert wrote many of them. In certain quarters, people will begin referring to you as "the New Schubert."

You may feel guilty stealing a line from Darwin, or someone else, but don't worry. Bob Dylan's been doing it for years, and he won the Nobel Prize!

Now you have one song in Serbo-Croatian and another co-written with Charles Darwin. Already you are the most innovative singer at your local open mike. Everyone else is writing songs like:

> Caroline,
> I'll never forget you,
> Though a valentine
> I never did get you.

That's an actual lyric by the songwriter Scott Beambo.

Now you have written two songs. It's time to perform a "cover" song. Here's how you do it: find an obscure song nobody has thought about in years, learn it, and sing it. Here's a suggestion: "Seven Brides" by the (fictional) rap group Fireflyy. Sample lyrics:

> Seven brides for seven brothers;
> Seven maids for seven mothers;
> Seven AIDS for seven lovers.
> Don't steal my head! Don't run the gutters!

Study the lyrics seven times, then sing it. This time, instead of holding a guitar, hold a didgeridoo.

Now it's time to write a political song. This is quite easy. Just find a blog post that you agree with, divide it into twelve-syllable lines, and throw in a few rhymes.

You now have four songs (including one cover). You are definitely a singer-songwriter!

How to Throw a Party

❀ ❀ ❀

One party can change the world. In this apolitical world of consumerism, the party represents an ideology perhaps more valid than the tenuous theory of human rights. The emerging field of "party theory" engages with the meaning of informal social gatherings.

Vladimir I. Lenin spoke about the importance of the party. He wrote:

> A party is the vanguard of a class, and its duty is to lead the masses and not merely to reflect the average political level of the masses. ["Speech On The Agrarian Question," November 14, 1917]

This concept is just as true for a private party as for a political one.

While I was living in Boulder, Colorado, in 1976, I met a guy—outside the Carnival Café—who said, "You should come over to our party."

"How long has it been going on?" I asked.

He thought for a moment. "About two years," he replied.

Here are some party ideas:

1) An all-animal party. Have your friends bring their canaries, goldfish, dogs, cats, pythons to your house. Gather all the animals in a room, and let them party. I would recommend having a fearless and strong person watching from a distance—perhaps through a window—in case intervention is necessary.

2) A string party. Invite people to bring string, thread, yarn, twine, or even dental floss to your house. Each person will tie a line around their waist, and secure the other end to a piece of furniture. As people walk through the party, these strings will become entwined. At a prearranged time—perhaps midnight—take out a pair of scissors and cut everyone free.

3) An indigestion party. This is a potluck where everyone is invited to bring indigestible food. After eating, partygoers lie on the floor (or on the sofa) and complain.

4) A money party. Each guest arrives with money—thirty-five cents, five dollars, $1,250—whatever they choose. All the money is piled in the center of a room. After fifteen minutes, guests may help themselves to the loot. See what happens!

5) Identical gathering. Include a dress code in your invitation: let's say, black slacks and a yellow top. All attendees must wear this uniform. Once the room is full, take lots of photos.

6) Silence soirée. In this party, no one speaks. Partiers are allowed to use sign language and other gestures. (Writing notes is prohibited.) Of course, everyone is free to dance.

7) Ridicule party. Choose one person by lot, and tease him (or her). The party ends when the person bursts into tears.

8) Praise party. Choose one person by lot, and praise her (or him). The party ends when the person bursts into tears (of gratitude).

9) Armenian party. Ask all your friends to learn Armenian. [Note: This may take six months.] When everyone is fluent, invite them to your house. Insist that all conversation be in Armenian. Serve Armenian delicacies while wearing traditional Armenian attire.

10) Nozzle party. Each partygoer must bring a nozzle of some kind. When the guests have arrived, stand around and compare nozzles.

I'm sure you can imagine party motifs of your own. Some will be duds, I predict. (Probably the "nozzle party" will fall into this category.) But others will be unexpected delights (e.g., the "insult party"). However you choose to party, never go to a party store. Any celebration decorated with party store items will end in tragedy.

Dance Your Way to Health

❂ ❂ ❂

Believe it or not, science has studied the health benefits of dancing. Dancing improves balance and coordination, muscle strength, flexibility—and increases metabolism. The most immediate improvement, I find, is to the back. Properly executed, gentle undulation relieves lower back distress.

Once you continuously move for twenty minutes, you receive the blessings of aerobic exercise, including cardiovascular enhancement and even better memory. And don't forget mental health. It's hard to be despondent while dancing.

A "dance doctor" examines the patient and prescribes particular movements to improve bodily functioning. Visit a dance doctor today! And here are some further tips:

Begin with video. Ask a friend to videotape your walk. Study the way your body habitually negotiates a sidewalk or country lane. Then elaborate these motions into a dance.

Dance a simple dance. I once heard an interview with jazz pianist Dave Brubeck, who said: "It took me a long time to learn, while composing, that no idea can be too simple." Follow this principle in your dancing. Don't be afraid to sway back and forth repetitively, or to slide one foot along the floor. Sometimes the most basic dance is the most salutary.

Recycle dances. Just as one recycles yogurt containers, so may one recycle movement strategies. I, for example, remember numerous dances of the 1960s: the Mashed Potato, the Hully Gully, the Freddie, the Twist—plus the surreal gyrations of Grateful Dead-lovers. All of these find expression in my personal locomotion. (Which reminds me, there was a dance song by Little Eva called "Do the Loco-Motion"!)

Try the Wall Dance. This is a freestyle movement in which you must touch a wall at all times, either with your whole body or just your toe or ass or elbow. Play a Czech folksong record and do the Wall Dance!

Use the two-radio method. Listen to two radios playing two different stations simultaneously. Now do a complex cha-cha to both stations at once!

Do the tapping dance. Yesterday, while I was meditating, I heard my wife tapping her entire body, from top to bottom. After a while, I realized she was actually typing on the keyboard of her laptop. But why don't you try that percussive movement I mistakenly heard—the head-to-toe tapping dance?

Divide your body in half. Dance forward with the left half of your body while your right side moves backwards. Now reverse!

Dance all day. I recommend that you dance three times a day, for six minutes at a time. But another option is to incorporate dance into your daily travels through the house. As you traverse the living room, weave from side to side, then wiggle and hop. (I do this often.) One delight is to walk as close to the wall as you can. Let your hallway graze your face!

Do the towel dance. Many daily household activities may be transformed into dances. Just as Gene Kelly spins classic movie magnetism by walking with an umbrella in *Singin' in the Rain*, try beginning a dance by toweling yourself off after a bath. And while showering, stomp to a 3/4 rhythm—a wet waltz. (Most showers are in 3/4; a bath is usually 2/4.)

And don't assume you must dance alone. Why not invite four or eight friends over to your house to share your bodily expression? (Having an odd number—including you—removes the tendency to dance in couples.) And don't just invite friends! Consider asking your enemies, also. Forty-seven minutes of frantic shimmying usually removes all animosity.

While you're waiting, dance. Train yourself to treat any delay as a dance invitation. As you stand on line at the supermarket, begin to whirl. (After all, music is playing, almost always.) With any luck, everyone else standing on line will join you—then the cashier! Then the store manager!

Why not start your own dance craze? Incidentally, there are still new dances, though people over the age of twenty-three rarely hear of them. One example is the "Kiki Challenge," based on a song by Drake. But you can also invent your own dancing styles. Here's one I created:

The Bungalow Bop

Come into my bungalow;
The ceiling's very low.
You have to lean over
And waddle to and fro.

Do the Bungalow Bop
In the kitchen;
Do the Bungalow Bop
In the pantry;
Do the Bungalow Bop-Bop-Bop!

Keep your elbows in;
Point your toes out;
Tilt your knees sideways,
As if you have gout.

Do the Bungalow Bop
In the daytime;
Do the Bungalow Bop
During playtime;
Do the Bungalow Bop-Bop-Bop!

Dances are largely ethnic. Choose a nation and imitate their dancing. For example, a short session on YouTube reveals that traditional Laotian dance emphasizes flowing hand gestures, seen in profile. Attempt that!

Don't forget feeling. Remember to imbue your private dance-spectacles with emotion. Let joy, fright, envy, desolation, amorousness find expression in your limbs.

Try juggling money as you twirl. Throw dollars into the air, and then snatch them back. Everyone loves to watch a money mambo.

Birds are inspirational for the footloose. Today, while waiting for the bus in Phoenicia, I gazed up at two slowly circling turkey vultures, then imitated their smooth dance. (Luckily no one was around to see.)

Try weights. The same way it's possible to run with weights, one may also dance with added burdens. My ninety-nine-year-old father scrupulously lifts weights daily—two cans of soup. While you dance, try gesticulating with Campbell's Minestrone in one hand and Progresso Chicken Noodle in the other—with a box of Ronzoni Spaghetti No. 8 strapped to each shin. Increase the gravitational undertow!

And don't forget hula hoops! They are an excellent accompaniment to domestic dancing. Search in your attic for one, or make your own, out of bent willow twigs bound together by milkweed stalks. (FYI, the average hula hoop is between forty and forty-four inches in diameter.) Rustic hula hoops will soon be a big trend, take my word for it.

[And check with your physician, acupuncturist, shaman—or all three—before implementing any of the suggestions I've given. I can't afford to be sued!]

The Slow Read Movement

✦ ✦ ✦

I moved from New York City to the hamlet of Phoenicia in 1998. Immediately, I became frustrated with the local "culture." Growing up in Manhattan, I was like a bee in the hive of that island. The humming of the other inhabitants informed me, reassured me. Now, walking alone among mist-draped mountains—with no one nearby speaking Polish, Italian, Puerto Rican, German, French, Chinese—I felt unnourished.

Luckily, Phoenicia has a first-rate thrift shop with a witty name: "Formerly Yours." The prices are extremely low—some pants cost a quarter—but there's also a free table, and among its items are books. Formerly Yours is the opposite of a New York City bookstore: you must pay for romance novels, but collections of Freudo-Marxist essays are free. One day, on the giveaway table, I found *Moby-Dick* (the Signet paperback, from 1978). Immediately I snapped it up. That night I lay in bed and opened my new acquisition:

> Call me Ishmael. Some years ago—never mind how
> long precisely—having little or no money in my
> purse, and nothing particular to interest me onshore,

> I thought I would sail about a little and see the
> watery part of the world.

It was elegant, stately, poetic—but who could read it? This
book demanded the intelligence of a Princeton professor and
the patience of St. Jerome. It's the goddamn Great American
Novel! *Moby-Dick*'s as intimidating as... a massive white
whale! Sadly, I cast the classic aside.

Three days later, however, I hit upon a plan. In Phoenicia,
there is infinite time. I knew that if I read a page a day, I'd
eventually finish this gargantuan novel. So I began. Each day
I read a section of the text, marking my progress with a pencil.
Melville became my spectral companion, speaking to me daily:

> Now, when I say that I am in the habit of going to
> sea whenever I begin to grow hazy about the eyes,
> and begin to be over conscious of my lungs, I did
> not mean to have it inferred that I ever go to sea as
> a passenger. For to go as a passenger you must needs
> have a purse, and a purse is but a rag unless you have
> something in it.

Moby-Dick is almost too great a book. Reading it burns
your eyes. When you're in the middle of an Agatha Christie
novel, you won't stop to eat—not even to drink a glass of water.
Reading Melville is the opposite. Every three sentences, you
must stare at the ceiling and wonder where your life went
wrong. It's the perfect book to read with tragical slowness.

One virtue of *Moby-Dick*: you're not going to forget the
plot. [Spoiler alert: It's about a bunch of guys on a whaling
ship, searching for a whale.] A startling discovery: the Great

American Novel is not set in America (except for a brief introduction)! It follows a route through the Atlantic, around Cape Horn, into the Indian Ocean, and on to the Pacific. Another discovery: Melville was such a visionary he wanted to SAVE THE WHALES one hundred and twenty years before that bumper sticker was written.

For six years I sailed on the *Pequod*, checking on the progress of my ship every night between 8:00 and 8:30 p.m. As a whaler slowly crosses the ocean, I reached page 150, then page 200, then page 238 … As Captain Ahab grew more obsessed with Moby-Dick, I grew more obsessed with *Moby-Dick*.

Some people skip the informational chapters on whaling, but not me. That would be like taking a shortcut in the Boston Marathon:

> Throughout the Pacific, and also in Nantucket, in New Bedford, and Sag Harbor, you will come across lively sketches of whales and whaling-scenes, graven by the fishermen themselves on Sperm Whale-teeth, or ladies' busks wrought out of the Right Whale-bone, and other like scrimshander articles, as the wheelman call the numerous little ingenious contrivances they elaborately carve out of the rough material, in their hours of ocean leisure.

[A "busk" is part of a corset.] In Chapter 95, Melville describes the penis of a whale the boat has slaughtered:

> Had you stepped on board the *Pequod* at a certain juncture of this post-mortemizing of the whale; and had you strolled forward nigh the windlass, pretty

sure am I that you would have scanned with no
small curiosity a very strange, enigmatical object,
which you would have seen there, lying along
lengthwise in the lee scuppers. Not the wondrous
cistern in the whale's huge head; not the prodigy
of his unhinged lower jaw; not the miracle of his
symmetrical tail; none of these would so surprise
you, as half a glimpse of that unaccountable cone,—
longer than a Kentuckian is tall, nigh a foot in
diameter at the base, and jet-black as Yojo, the ebony
idol of Queequeg.

It's possible that Melville went a little bit insane writing
the book. Here is Ahab speaking in Chapter 108 (angry that
he must wait for the carpenter to fashion him a new pegleg):

Oh, Life! Here I am, proud as Greek God, and yet
standing debtor to this blockhead for a bone to
stand on! Cursed be that mortal inter-indebtedness
which will not do away with ledgers. I would be free
as air; and I'm down in the whole world's books. I
am so rich, I could have given bid for bid with the
wealthiest praetorians at the auction of the Roman
Empire (which was the world's); and yet I owe for
the flesh in the tongue I brag with. By heavens!

Just as the "Slow Food Movement" reverses the momentum
of modern life, emphasizing local ingredients and long meal
preparation, my Slow Read Movement pulled me back into
the thoughtfulness of a world of lamps filled with ... whale
oil!

I didn't know how the book would end. I never saw the 1956 film with Gregory Peck, and no one at a party ever said: "Weren't you surprised at the ending of *Moby-Dick*? I couldn't believe Ishmael went off with that mermaid!"* After six years of reading, I reached the conclusion: "And the great shroud of the sea rolled on as it rolled five thousand years ago." With vigorous, sustained mental effort, I'd conquered Melville! If I can do it, so can you. Find a weighty book, a sharp pencil, and join the Slow Read Movement!

*I'm not saying this is the actual plot of the book.

Fifty-Three Steps to Invigorated Aging

1) As you age, your life contains more nouns and less verbs. The books and trophies on your shelves grow heavier, dustier. You must fight the inertia of time. Verbify yourself! I once read that the average housewife walks 2.3 miles a day just around her house. This strongly influenced me. I decided to hike as much as possible in my apartment, to constantly manufacture new tasks for myself. Now I spend my day sharpening pencils, washing two or three dishes, beginning to make the bed and then remembering a poem I've composed but haven't transcribed, such as:

Sad Truth

> I searched for
> love but all I found
> was happiness.

—then pacing over to my computer to write it down. Then I hop up again, to clear off the kitchen table!

2) Be willing to look old. Aged faces can be iconic. We live
in a culture that despises superannuated people but loves
antiques—a tragic paradox. Try to resemble a Victorian
lampshade.

3) Writing palindromes is the secret to mental youthfulness.
(A palindrome is a word, phrase, or Supreme Court decision
that reads the same backwards and forwards.) At night in bed,
just before falling asleep, I often practice this genial art form.
Here are some recent palindromic compositions:

> Noses on!
> Tipsy, my spit.
> No! Help pin a nipple, hon!
> Do not refer to Nod.
> Blurt out: "Tuotrulb!"
> Da, Lassie is salad.
> In words drown I.
> No, man; nice cinnamon!
> Sex is sixes.

Thinking in two directions at once strengthens both halves
of the brain.

4) Vary your walking speed. Walk slowly and thoughtfully, like
a rhinoceros, for a while—then skitteringly, like a sandpiper.

5) **Strategy for Aging**

> When
> I get
> dementia,
> my poems
> will
> improve.

6) Touch trees. Humans have faces in the front, but trees have 360-degree faces. Close your eyes and learn the Braille of a tree's skin.

7) Play the tonette every day. Do you know what a tonette is? It's a plastic, flute-like instrument that essentially anyone can play. My tonette has seven holes, plus one in the back, which seems to add an octave. I only use mine outdoors. (In my opinion, music should be unconfined by houses.) I live between a mountain and a creek. The mountain is called Romer Mountain. The creek is called the Esopus. I walk outside, usually in the afternoon, and play my tonette for two or three minutes: quick avant-garde noodlings, or methodical sequences that sound like music exercises for eight-year-olds.

A bad musician is still a musician. Though I have no "talent," I am still a tonette player! No one can deny that!

8) Cook happy food.

Some food is inherently happy. Today I made a salad: romaine lettuce, sliced red pepper, fresh green beans, black olives, artichoke hearts. This is happy food. (Incidentally, I find that I require at least one salad a day for fine health.)

9) But also prepare other types of food!

Food, like art, should be various. Just as you wouldn't want to see only orange paintings, you don't want to eat only happy foods. You need nonhappy foods, too. Learn to cook solemn breakfasts, quizzical lunches, zealous suppers.

10) Develop your memory.

Try to remember all the presidents with mustaches. (Hint: There were only four, and they were virtually in a row!)

11) One way to stay warm in winter: walk outside.

My wife and I keep our house quite cold in the winter—sometimes as low as fifty degrees. But if I'm cold, I just walk outside. I return invigorated, plus the house will briefly seem distinctly warm.

Violet and I get sick much less than other people, by living in the cold. Americans drive themselves into illness through heating and air-conditioning. Which reminds me:

12) Cure a cold with potatoes.

Around 1980 I discovered the cure for the common cold: fried potatoes. French fries work best, but potato chips will suffice, if necessary. I have no idea why this works, but I passed this remedy on to my daughter Sylvia, who endorses it.

13) Do yoga with your hands.

Study a book—or website—of yoga postures, and reproduce them with your hands. Do the "downward dog" with your left hand, while your right hand performs the "sun salutation." This will add 3.7 years to your life.

14) Grow wise. Most experts on aging advise "staying young," but that's nonsense. The youthful are young; that's their talent. The aged should, instead, grow deep in wisdom.

How do you become wise? I have no idea.

15) Learn to fail. Most of us attempt to get better and better at our hobbies and careers. We want to improve as tennis players, as firefighters, as sushi chefs. But what we forget is that failure is also a talent—often a more adaptive talent than success. Life is mostly a series of defeats, which usually catch us unawares. But if you willfully undertake projects at which you're destined to fail—designing a solar-powered rocket ship, for example—you'll develop the strength necessary to live for years and years and years. So choose a task you'll never do well and start trying. Attempt to master backgammon or to cure cancer. It's up to you. (And possibly, just by dumb luck, you'll build a solar-powered rocket ship!)

16) Love your bacteria. We speak of a wine aging, or a cheese, or anything that is catalyzed by bacteria. Well, guess what? Humans are one or two percent bacteria, by weight. That means that if you weigh a hundred and sixty pounds, you're carrying around nearly two pounds of single-celled organisms, mostly in your intestines and on your skin. Forget about your "Inner Child"; consider your "Inner City" of bacteria. Study your own microbial colony; learn what these beneficial creatures enjoy. Buy a jar of artichoke hearts, place a few in your salad, eat them, and notice how your bacteria react. Are they delighted? Insulted? Try other foods. (In theory, they should respond to miso soup, yogurt, kefir, red wine, and other foodstuffs that include bacteria, but your particular bacterial subculture may

have its own preferences.) Co-evolving with your microbes is the happiest way to age.

17) Study your date of birth. The older you get, the more you become an emissary from a vanished world—in my case, a world of black-and-white photographs taken by a Brownie camera, the sun bleaching the faces of the squinting subjects. In particular, what happened the day you were born? On my birthday, French forces in Vietnam cornered a brigade of the Vietminh in the Red River Delta. A Canadian boat captain died as a German freighter sank after colliding with a Great Lakes ore carrier in the St. Clair River on a moonless night. Hysteria gripped Dallas as the rapist-killer of Mrs. H. C. Parker eluded police. A three-man board of inquiry opened a hearing on the dock strike that was crippling the Eastern seaboard. President Eisenhower had a sore elbow, "painful and annoying," but nothing to worry about, according to Press Secretary James C. Hagerty. The Dodgers beat the Yankees 3–2 in the World Series. Red Skelton was on the cover of *TV Guide* (which cost fifteen cents).

18) Now you are a historian. You have certain duties, as a curator of memories. Suppose you were in Cleveland in 1982. Read a book about that period. Reflect on it. Write an essay about your own life in Cleveland in '82, and how it contradicts that book. Post it on your Instagram account. Someday a graduate student may read your entry and slap her forehead.

19) Do everything as slowly as possible. Orr, a character in *Catch-22*, believed he would live longer by doing tedious, repetitive tasks, like taking apart a radio and putting it back together.

For example, when you leave the bathtub, dry yourself so slowly that most of the water just evaporates. If you live slowly enough, one hour becomes three hours and twenty minutes.

20) Sing archaic songs like:

> In Dublin's fair city, where girls are so pretty
> I first set my eyes on sweet Molly Malone
> As she wheeled her wheelbarrow
> Through streets broad and narrow
> Crying: "Cockles and mussels, alive, alive-O!
> Alive, alive-O! alive, alive-O!"
> Crying: "Cockles and mussels, alive, alive-O!"

As you age, you have a right to such songs; it is delightful to see a man with a flowing white beard, or a woman with deep wrinkles, sing "Molly Malone." It reaffirms one's faith in the fragile human race.

21) Read joke books. I found *The Treasury of Clean Jokes for Children* by Tal D. Bonham on the free shelf of the Phoenicia thrift shop, so I took it home. Here's a joke I opened to at random:

> **Brandon:** Today on the school bus a little boy fell off his seat, and everybody laughed except me.
> **Teacher:** Who was the little boy?
> **Brandon:** Me.

This joke has the virtue of also being a Buddhist parable. (Come to think of it, this could be one way to become wise: reading joke books.)

22) Invent new methods of meditation. There are at least forty-three thousand traditional methods of silent contemplation. Think of some new ones yourself. For example:

> Close your eyes. Pay attention to your breathing. Now picture an anthill—see it as clearly as possible. As you breathe in, envision three hundred and six ants entering the anthill. As you breathe out, see three hundred and five ants exiting the anthill. Now breathe in; watch three hundred and five ants enter the hill. Breathe out; see three hundred and hour ants leaving. Continue until the anthill is full.

23) Learn new words. I am constantly writing down words I don't know as I read. Later I search for their definitions and write them in a little notebook with a tiger-skin cover. (Don't worry, vegans, it's not real tiger skin!) Here are my most recent words:

> **refractometer:** an instrument for measuring a refractive index
> **billycock:** felt hat
> **plethoric:** superabundant
> **tonneau:** rear seating compartment of an early type of automobile
> **casements:** window sashes that open outward by means of hinges
> **perfusion:** injection of fluid into a blood vessel

24) Make birthday cards for your friends. It's quite simple. Think of a famous person the recipient will be impressed

by, and type that name into your search engine, followed by "quotes." [For example: "Elizabeth Cady Stanton quotes."] Then choose one of the more obscure quotations and illustrate it with a drawing of a covered bridge. (It doesn't matter if you're the world's worst artist; everyone is impressed by a picture of a covered bridge.) For example, I made my mother a birthday card yesterday, for which I chose a quote from Jane Austen: "The person, be it gentleman or lady, who has not pleasure in a good novel, must be intolerably stupid"—accompanied by a drawing of the author.* (Jane came out a little gaunt, but lovely.) All this on handmade rice paper my friend Dan gave to me!

Of course, your beneficiary may not appreciate your gesture, but the pleasure of making a card—and of saving money and joining the "creative class"—is independent of the work's reception. (Besides, your next card may be better!)

*On rare occasions, one may depict something besides a covered bridge.

25) Speaking of Jane Austen, books exist in profusion. There are enough great books to entertain you for the next thirteen thousand years. And reading is a pleasure that only deepens with age. As your physical mobility lessens, your mental mobility increases. When it becomes too taxing to visit China, lay back with Cao Xueqin's eighteenth-century masterpiece, *Dream of the Red Chamber*!

26) Remember, miracles are real. Every year, over sixteen hundred medical miracles are recorded—in Canada alone!* Cancer sufferers are suddenly cured; arthritis disappears. Do

these miracles come from God? No one knows. Possibly they are the work of Mike Pence. But the point is: Never lose hope!

*I invented this statistic.

27) Take a nap. Napping is an art, like ceramics. A great nap can reinvent a day. You awake to clearer, fresher air—*happier* air. And old people are allowed to nap—it's considered basically a virtue.

28) Go walking in the woods. The Japanese have a word for a nature walk: *Shinrin-yoku*, which is translated as "forest bathing." Scientific studies show that forest bathing reduces stress, anger, insomnia and anxiety. (Really!) Find nearby—or distant—woodlands and hike. The best weather is a light mist, just less than a drizzle, when the leaves sparkle with aerial-sexual energy.

29) Try every kind of therapy—or to be more precise, every therapy you can afford. Recently I visited my friend Karen Charman, who is now a certified BioSET, Body Code, and EFT practitioner. We were doing a Body Code session, and she asked my Subconscious a series of questions, then gauged my responses by testing the energy flow through my arm muscle. In other words, she had me hold out my arm, posed a question, then pushed it down. (Sample question: "Is Sparrow feeling grief?") If the answer was no, my arm wouldn't budge, but if it was yes, the arm could easily be lowered. In this way, she learned about my "heart wall," an energetic barrier around my chest consisting of anxieties and fears. She would locate the precise problem—for example, "fear of failure"—then go

behind me and roll a magnet down my spine. (The magnet had spikes and felt like a pastry wheel for cutting pastry dough.) If it was a small blockage, she would roll the magnet five times; for a larger blockage, twenty rolls were necessary. Karen continued clearing energy imbalances for about an hour. Afterwards I felt fabulous—almost immortal. The Body Code is illogical to me, but it works!

30) Make new friends and have tea with them. Coffee is for chatting; tea is for *real* talk. (Coffee suggests a "coffee break," a rushed, finite time. Tea is timeless.)

31) Ask for help. All of us need assistance, and as we age, we need more of it. By the time you're seventy-nine, you'll need more friends than ever! So start asking for help—with cooking, cleaning, dog-grooming. Ask young people, but also ask the aged; even people older than yourself! (Three hundred octogenarians can lift a car, easily, if they act together.)

I have a friend—I'll call him Portsmouth Pete—who, in his youth, would ask every single woman at a party to have sex with him. More often than you'd expect, one would say yes—a complete stranger! (His ratio of success was approximately 1:26.) Once you are aged, you need the same spirit of blithe request. Who knows why someone may wish to help you? Perhaps their guru instructed them to. Perhaps they're incredibly bored. Or maybe they're plagued by guilt because they recently robbed a bank. In any case, there's no harm in asking. And don't be bitter if they say no. Notice if this 1:26 ratio still holds.

32) Start a garden! In England, the elderly all have little garden plots where they spend hours silently (and sometimes audibly) speaking to their green cousins.* No wonder Britain produces great poets!

*According to geneticists, a human has 35 percent of the same DNA as a daisy.

33) Find a painless person to love. Most love requires sacrifice and suffering, but certain individuals are perfectly safe to adore from afar. Choose from this list (or, if you insist, you may supply your own candidate):

> The Dalai Lama
> Jennifer Lawrence
> Frank Zappa
> Socrates
> Susan Sontag

Spend about three minutes a day fervently loving this person.

34) Buy ironic clothes. Once you are older than fifty, it's perfectly acceptable to wear a shirt with pictures of large toucans on it, or a cartoony bowling ball. You may wear a necktie if you're a woman or a tiara if you're a man. Your clothing says: "At my age, I can dress as queerly as I choose; the foolish Laws of Fashion no longer confine me!"

35) Or become a spy. On days that you're not in the mood to dress bizarrely, wear nondescript clothes and pass through the world unnoticed. Age is a kind of camouflage. You're no threat

to anyone, so strangers will act without restraint—yell at their kids, passionately kiss, sing to themselves—right before your eyes. Enjoy the great theatre of human life!

36) Floss your teeth twice a day. People worry about their teeth when they should be worrying about their gums. Gums are the soil in which teeth are planted. Cultivate your gums, and your gums will nourish their enamel brothers. There are numerous intriguing projects to pursue while flossing. One excellent option is to listen to music. (Currently I'm listening to *The Best of Ray Charles*—a real record album, not the product of a "streaming service," which I bought when I was sixteen, in 1969.) Certain friends don't mind conversing with you while you floss your teeth; others find it repulsive. Through investigation, you will sort your friends into these two groups. Also, you may read a flat magazine; it's trickier to read a book—though it's possible to prop one open with a brick or an andiron.

37) Also, buy a dental stimulator. I know it's an unnerving quasi-sexual phrase, but this inexpensive item—a metal rod, about the size of a pen, with a rubber tip—is more valuable than a thousand saunas.

38) Seltzer! Seltzer is essentially Coca-Cola without the sugar, chemicals, or caffeine. In 1911 many Eastern Europeans believed this liquid aided digestion, prevented constipation, and improved all health. Nowadays, no one accepts these claims—except you! Drink small amounts of seltzer whenever possible: not religiously, but *seriously*. Notice, especially, the effects on your digestive system. (Also, use it to remove stains!)

39) Two poems

In Defense of Aging

The more
farsighted
I get,
the closer
are the stars.

Time Traveler

I'm a Time
Traveler:

I've traveled
from 1953
to 2020.

40) Use a magnifying glass to light a cigarette butt. This requires concentration and a hot, sunny day, but once you succeed, you will *understand* fire.

41) Perform two mutually contradictory actions. For example, play the piano while combing your hair. This will greatly improve your dexterity!

42) The best part of getting old is that you can stop worrying about becoming famous. Until you're twenty-four, there's a chance you'll be a celebrity, even if you're completely talentless. But as time goes on, that possibility diminishes, and by the time you're seventy-one, it's infinitesimal. Also, you'll have lost touch with that Inner Circle. When you open *People* magazine,

you've never heard of any of the stars (okay, maybe two out of eighty). There's a whole new pantheon of good-looking, empty-headed people with interchangeable names like Ryan Fletcher and Owen Basil, as unknowable as Polynesian deities. Besides, you're already famous in your neighborhood, or in your occupation—known as a trustworthy orthodontist in Northern Long Island or an excellent social worker in Arkansas—and that's good enough. Instead, you root for one of your grandsons to become world-famous.

43) The older I get, the more I admire Zen Buddhism. When I was a teenager, I'd read a koan like this one and be completely baffled:

Pick up a stone deep in the ocean with dry hands.

After turning fifty-five, I found that such paradoxes began to make sense. There's an essential duality in the nature of life—between what I want and what I can achieve—that is beginning to penetrate my knobby skull. I have even, at stray moments, heard the sound of one hand clapping—a voiceless thump—while walking in a meadow, or in downtown St. Louis. I'm not exactly a Zen Buddhist; I'm just old, which is almost the same thing. The mask I was born with is beginning to crack.

44) Improve your breathing. Most of us are either in-breathers or out-breathers. That is, we tend to emphasize inhalation or exhalation. If you prefer to breathe in, work on exhaling. If you're an out-breather, cultivate the in-breath. Try to balance the two tides of respiration.

45) Remember, you're living space as well as time. Calculate, as best you can, how far you've traveled across the Earth's surface. Instead of saying, "I am seventy-eight years old," say, "I am 620,000 miles old."

46) Listen to dance. My friend Yumeko and I went to a free dance performance in Central Park of two groups: Complexions Contemporary Ballet and Carolyn Dorfman Dance. At the entrance, we found a barricade and a guard saying: "We've reached capacity." In other words, we couldn't get in. So Yumeko and I sat on the lawn outside listening to the dance. Surprisingly, others were near us, also being entertained by invisible dancers. At first, we heard a solo cello playing classical music, then African-American gospel singing (I think), then a live, heavy metal band (I think; Yumeko recognized two Metallica songs). Though, unfortunately, we couldn't hear the dancers' feet thumping on the stage, we could picture black-clad performers in leotards clambering up metal lattices, or a woman in a long silvery gown slowly forming her body into the letter *C*. What better way to combat senility than to sit outside a dance performance imagining its choreography?

47) Bake. A baker creates a community—so become a baker; be one of those grandmothers (even if you have no grandchildren) who spread sweetness in the form of circular pastries. Or one of the grandfathers! If you're male, don't be ashamed to tie on an apron!

Once in a while, bake muffins with no refined sugar, sweetened only with dates or ripe bananas. See if anyone notices they're eating "health muffins."

48) Improve your balance. Find a fallen log and balance on it. Then balance on a boulder, then a park bench—then a mailbox! Happy balancing is the key to successful aging. Begin your Balance Studies now!

49) Go on a two-day screen fast. During that time, avoid televisions, iPhones, iPads, computers. See if the actual physical world becomes more vivid—and if you sleep better, without funny cat videos replaying endlessly inside your skull.

50) Make a list of all your failings. For example, here's a list of mine:

1. I have a terrible memory.
2. I have no mechanical ability whatsoever—for example, I could never fix a toaster.
3. I am lazy.
4. I am awful at learning languages.
5. I'm a very slow reader.
6. I can barely cook.
7. I dress like a slob.
8. I never remember anyone's birthday.
9. I am narcissistic.
10. I'm a very poor swimmer.
11. I have no sense of etiquette.
12. I dislike Christmas.

I'll stop there. Post your list on your refrigerator, and consult it daily. How will you improve, if you don't honestly assess yourself?

51) Stand up for your beliefs. There's nothing like a ninety-three-year-old woman at an antiracism rally to bring tears to everyone's eyes. Be that person.

52) Give advice. As you grow wiser, more and more people will ask you for advice. Your nephew—or grandnephew—will ask, "Should I go to graduate school?" You must reply, even if you have no answer. One possibility is to follow Jesus's example—invent a meaningless parable. Say: "A farmer had a field. She planted half of it with barley and half with corn. Within the barley, some corn sprang up, but among the corn, no barley grew." Then sit back, smiling enigmatically. [Notice the non-sexist language. One should always aspire to be less sexist than Jesus.]

53) Stop reading self-help books. They're making us all so stupid, we can barely finish reading a self-help book!

PART 5

Brief Epiphanies

MISTER
FLOSSY

Think of your grandmother. Picture her as clearly as you can. Then picture *her* grandmother. Then picture *her* grandmother. In your mind, see this chain of grandmothers stretching back to prehistory.

A long line of blessed grandmothers!

We are raised by our mothers but sustained by our grandmothers.

Write down the numbers one through twelve on a piece of paper, one number to a line. Then as quickly as possible write down, next to each number, the first word that enters your mind. Don't stop to think at all!

Now carefully look at your twelve words.

Here, let me show you my results:

1. pull
2. clack
3. Henry
4. bejesus
5. crack
6. small
7. open
8. cough
9. smee
10. sweet
11. doorpost

12. Howard

What can we learn from this weird sequence? In my haste to think quickly, I invented a word, "smee," which I quickly amended to "sweet." Perhaps "smee" is the key to my entire psyche. But what exactly does it mean? It's a short word, containing the word "me." It sounds a little smeary, almost slimy. It's the slimy form of the word "me." Do I see myself as smeary, even smelly?

And who is Henry? And more importantly, who is Howard? Because possibly the last word in the series is the most essential. Henry and Howard seem like gentle, inoffensive male persons. Perhaps they are my future friends? Do I yearn for friends, to improve my smelly, smeary self?

See how the easy this is, to understand one's entire life through twelve quickly written words?

I like to go walking—not to walk, but to *see*. Why don't you try this harmless diversion? Go on a seeing tour—but don't forget to listen, also. You may hear thrilling techno music from passing cars, or screams from inside houses.

Pick up a leaf from the ground and cradle it. Give it a name. (I picked up an acacia leaf and named it Abele (pronounced "Abba-lee").

Worrying does not help. It doesn't make anyone stronger or prouder. Try to guide your mind into non-worrying. Filling your life with silly games is much preferable to filling your life

with gruesome anxieties. Spinning a top is better than growing panic-stricken about, for instance, the next presidential
election. (Unless you *volunteer* to work in the next congres-
sional election. Action is excellent. It's even better at killing
worry than top-spinning.)

Think of a country you'd like to visit. Research that nation,
preferably using books, not a computer. Make a list of salient
facts about your destination. Pack a suitcase full of clothing
appropriate to that climate. Place it in your closet.

Everyone needs an exit strategy.

The first self-help books were written by God.

Punch the Earth. Go to a lawn or meadow or vacant lot and
punch the ground, hard as you can. You may do so angrily or
mechanically, it's up to you. Give the Earth two or three hard
jabs. Then walk away, muttering to yourself.

Your goal is not complete happiness, but rather the very edge
of happiness. Let others seek one hundred percent joy; for you,
the rim of happiness is enough.

In order to help others, it's necessary to spend a certain amount
of time daydreaming.

God speaks to us through diseases. God says: "Don't eat so
much meat! Walk, run, bicycle, swim! Don't overeat! Get

plenty of sleep. Avoid white sugar. Live a simple life, with many friends!"

But we don't listen to God. Instead we go to the doctor, and take more pills.

No baby is born with the urge to watch videos. For them, life itself is sufficient.

Orthodox Jews have complex dietary rules known as kosher laws. Create your own dietary restrictions: for example, never eat Jell-O with quiche.

Wisdom wants to reach you, but you must invite Her.* After you wake in the morning, lie in bed for three minutes and speak to Wisdom: "Please come to my room!" And perhaps She will.

*Wisdom is not exactly a woman, but is a feminine force.

The next time you wash your hands, whether it's to prevent spreading coronavirus or simply for good hygiene, make up a little handwashing song, like:

> All my hands
> are only two:
> left, right;
> right, left.

Sing it as you wash.

Choose a book you don't like and start reading it. You need not study the entire work; just sample it. Feel the discomfort of reading an unloved book.

(I just looked through *The Ultimate Pet Lovers Joke Book* by Larry Wilde, and found:

> Why are there more sparrows than squirrels?
> Because screwing in the trees is for the birds!

What does that even *mean?*)

Unroll a sleeping bag on your floor, and lie on top of it. (On top of it, not in it.) Now think of every cat you've ever met. Remember their faces, and their names. This will improve your "cat memory."

Find the place in your body where you store resentment and anger. For me, as for many, it's my belly. In the 1970s, I would visualize a huge derrick lifting wreckage out of my belly on a metal chain. I spent hours and hours in 1979 picturing rusted girders being ripped from my midriff.

It seemed to help.

Joy is the type of love that requires no partner.

Hold a bowl in one hand, then drop a coin in it. Make sure you hold the bowl in midair, so the sound is clear. Over and over, experiment with this musical sound.

By the end of this book, you will be dancing to that music.

Imagine you could paint a new face on the moon. Which face would you choose? The next time you go to a shopping mall, look around and decide whose face should be superimposed on the moon.

Gravity reminds us that the Earth is below, pulling. The Earth *needs* us.

If you don't believe in God, try praying to the *New York Times*:

> O *New York Times*, send me a warm wind this afternoon!

I have found this to be extraordinarily effective.

Wait for winter, and walk around in snow. Listen to the odd little squinching sounds snow makes under your feet.

The Requirements

> You don't need "poetic
> talent" to write a poem.

> All you need is courage.

Go through all your clothing and find an item you'd like to

discard—but wear it for a day first. Have one last "fling" with your doomed garment.

Walk around with supreme self-confidence for half an hour. (If that's too long, try fifteen minutes.) If your self-assurance begins to flag, remind yourself that this is just an exercise. After the time elapses, return to your habitual uncertainty and self-doubt.

Eventually, try this practice once a month. Just think: You'll have six hours of confidence a year!

Sleep as much as possible. Sleep is entirely underrated in American society. If you have a bad sex life but a good sleep life, you're much healthier than vice versa.

Don't just celebrate your birthday. Try to intuit the day of your death, and celebrate that, too.

Try living your life one day at a time. Once you've accomplished that, start living half a day at a time. Then an eighth of a day at a time. Finally, live your life forty-seven minutes at a time.

Can a nation fart?

Do you floss your teeth? Well, if you don't, you probably should. And if you do, you have five to ten minutes a day—because I floss twice a day—to improve your mind. Today I flossed while visiting the grounds of the Riversdale House Museum, an historic mansion in Riverdale Park, Maryland. I watched robins hopping on the grass and contemplated the ugly main building, with its block-like Federalist style. I imagined I was a slave gazing at my master's house, intimidated by its stoic grandeur. (The Riversdale estate was originally a plantation.) Then I finished my flossing and moved on.

Spend a day dressed in judge's robes. Find a costume store to supply you with this singular attire, and go through your daily activities—even if you are a refrigerator mechanic—dressed in a long black robe. Notice how strangers react.

Study nutrition. Eat nutritious food. But don't be fanatical. Have a few potato chips once in a while. (And of course, popcorn is a purely natural food, unless you salt it to death).

Dates that cost no money:

> Going to a McDonald's and watching people eat.
> Sitting in a church and kissing passionately.
> Waiting on line at a railroad station.

Just now I saw a man on the subway twiddling one thumb—not both thumbs, just a single thumb. I didn't know this was possible! Why don't you try it? Take twenty seconds and twiddle one thumb.

No one has ever precisely measured a rainbow.

My friend Dan came to my house, so I made him a cup of
Yogi Tea. On his teabag was written:

> In every
> moment of life,
> you should be
> what you ought
> to be.

No wonder everyone hates the New Age!

The next time you feel an itch somewhere on your body, don't
immediately scratch it. Wait nine or ten seconds. Let the itch
beg you a little.

Certain people are here on Earth to help you. These are your
allies. You will know them when you see them. They usually
have glittering eyes.

Adopt the fifty-eight-minute hour. Here's how it works. Every
hour, use fifty-eight minutes for useful tasks. Then allow yourself two minutes to do anything you like: study astronomy,
play hopscotch, light a candle and blow it out, whistle. You'll
be happier, more efficient—and you may become a gifted
astronomer.

Lavish Mailbox

Don't buy a house:
just buy a mailbox,
and spend $30,000
renovating it until
it's the most lavish
mailbox.

That's all you need:
not a house, just
a beautiful mailbox.

If you find an ant in your house, give it a massage—but very, very gently.

Write a shopping list, then copy it. Exactly duplicate your previous writing. This will help if one day you decide to forge checks.

[Note: Only in rare circumstances is it ethical to forge checks.]

One of the few spiritual truths uttered by the Rolling Stones is in "You Can't Always Get What You Want," when they sing: "if you try sometime," you'll get exactly what you need.

I agree, but I would substitute "if you stop trying."

The merciful universe hovers over us like a mother penguin feeding her child regurgitated squid. There's no reason to try; you need simply to open your mouth.

For married people:

Remember, you can fall in love with everyone you meet, as long as you don't have sex with them.

For the unmarried:

You can fall in love with everyone you meet *and* have sex with them.

Probably you should be in therapy. Let me explain. You know how people nowadays often belong to a health club so they can exercise their bodies? You need a place to exercise your seventeen emotions.

And how do you choose a therapist? The same way you choose a mattress. You want one who's firm but comfortable. Just as a soft bed causes backache, a soft therapist weakens your core values.

The path to damnation is nice and straight. The path to wisdom twists and turns.

One of my favorite stories is about Charlie Parker, the magnificent jazz saxophonist. (I read it in *People* magazine.) Charlie was at a jazz club, and he turned to his girlfriend: "That bass player is great!"

"What are you talking about?" she replied. "He's awful!"

"You should've heard him two weeks ago," Bird replied.

The moral is: Don't try to be *good*. Just try to be better than you were two weeks ago.

Be patient with yourself—and even more patient with your nephews.

Through this book, you and I are becoming friends.

Find new ways to spend money. For example, suppose the next item you purchase costs twenty-three dollars. Throw a twenty-dollar bill and three singles up in the air. Let them float for a moment, then push them in four directions. Finally, with one grand sweep of your arm, gather them up and hand them to the sales clerk!

Don't allow anyone else to define success for you. In fact, don't even define it for yourself. Take a shit job and perform it with 100 percent devotion.

Turn shit into inspiration.

If everyone laughs at you, so what? What's so bad about laughter?

The next time you buy stamps at the post office, closely examine the designs first. Choose one that personally affects you: tulips (if you love tulips) or Daffy Duck. The type of stamps you buy is no small decision.

Forget the future.
Try to fix the past.

Most of us choose stable misery over mutable happiness.

I once shook hands with a man who had shaken hands with
W. H. Auden. Seek out people who've met your heroes.

If you find yourself in a house with a handmade rug, stare at it
for a while. There are secret messages in carpets. For example,
you may see a diamond with a three-pronged hat. What could
this mean?

   Someone spent a year making that carpet. Pay attention to
their symbology.

Write a fictitious Yellow Pages. Invent names and phone
numbers for dentists, plumbers, health clubs, nail salons,
pharmacies.

Throw a blanket into the air so that, just for a moment, it
resembles a bison.

Buy a treasure chest, place some valuables inside, and bury it.
Even if it only contains eighteen dollars, some future kid will
be thrilled to find it.

Share your grief with those less aggrieved than you.

Think of something you want—a horse, a violin, inner peace*— and sketch a picture of it. The picture may be hasty, or quite detailed. Then wait forty days. See if that item appears. This is known as a "sketch-prayer."

*It's quite simple to draw inner peace: just make a straight line inside a circle.

Before each meal, recite the following "grace":

> From elsewhere, we came here.
> From here, we will go elsewhere.
> All hail, transportation!

(Or make up your own grace.)

Think in black and white; live in color.

Next time you buy a pizza pie, give away a slice to someone standing around.

Go into a bus station and sit for three minutes. (Don't buy any food.) Notice the mood of the room. If you see a downtrodden person, tell them a joke.

Here's a sample joke:

> "Knock knock."
> "Who's there?"
> "Deja."
> "Deja who?"
> "Knock knock."

Get used to death. It is continual. It just hasn't hit you yet.

Find a rock band you've never heard of, preferably one from forty years ago. Listen to two of their songs. Go out and take a walk on a country lane. Think about that band. Where did they go wrong? What were their mistakes?

Invent a game without rules. Call it "plopjuice," or something like that. Spend an afternoon playing plopjuice.

If you were a superhero, what sort of hideout would you build?

The next time you go to the beach, drink some sea water. In small quantities, the sea is nourishing.

Your most cherished dreams will never come true—but you may achieve someone *else's* dreams.

Let the phone ring over and over once in a while, just to hear its plaintive cry.

Fight for what you believe in. If you don't know what you believe in, guess.

Remember, love is sometimes brief. You can fall in love for just thirteen minutes.

Never turn a Friday into a Thursday, or a Tuesday into a Sunday—even if you're under quarantine.

Walk through a city searching for a cyclops.

If you start to get a little sick, don't push yourself. Lie in bed and let idleness cure you.

Each generation of birds reinvents song.

The more yoga you do, the more yoga there *is* to do.

Become friends with your broom. Learn its eccentricities. Once you are intimate, caress its handle.

  You must sweep from time to time, so befriend your broom!

Actions speak louder than inactions.

Take a sad song and make it sadder.

When it rains for days and days, mushrooms rejoice.

Duct tape works just as well as thread for repairing torn clothes. You can even—using a skillful pair of scissors—darn socks with tape.

Stand in a corner of your living room and remember all your dead friends. (If you have no deceased comrades, think of great persons from the past: Descartes, Jane Austen, Isadora Duncan.) Send out greetings to these people, through the veil of death.

Wash a dollar bill, then iron it until it's completely flat. Try to make the dollar "new" again.

Sing deliberately off key, especially the notes C and F.

You can eat a salmon but you can't eat her soul.

Look through your closet and find clothing that makes you look like a foreigner. Wear it for two days. Notice if people talk extra loudly to you.

Buy local. Sell global.

After gazing at a glorious sunset, close your eyes. Try to *hear* the sunset.

Odd as it seems, two folksingers can despise each other.

Start a committee with nine friends. Meet twice a week for a month and gradually decide on a purpose for your committee. In the meantime, eat potato chips, chatter, and laugh.

A puddle evaporates, but the sea does not.

Make a toe ring out of leather. Wear it for two weeks, then decide if you like it.

Spend an afternoon trying to dematerialize. If you're still physically present after three hours, give up.

A backpack can sit on a chair, just like a person. Backpacks have a talent for sitting.

I once worked at a construction site outside Ithaca, New York. Every day I would eat lunch with a guy named Jerry. We'd eat together, talk, then Jerry would fall asleep. Exactly at the moment the lunch break was over, Jerry would awaken. If you can develop that talent, do so.

It's hard to wiggle your ears, but even more difficult to wiggle someone else's ears.

Choose a ringtone that everyone around you will love, even if you hate it. This is called selflessness.

Make an ancient friend: Cleopatra or Hesiod or Chuang Tzu. Learn as much as you can about your distant comrade. Write a letter (on parchment) to your ancient friend.

A good actor has three hundred distinct smiles.

Find a word you love and write it on your belt. (If you prefer the word to be secret, use the inside of your belt.)

Wouldn't it be great if houses had roofs that could open up in sunshine, then close again just before a rain?

Build such a house.

Never lie to yourself or to your therapist. Lie to your boss and to your mother.

Think of new ways to mispronounce your name. Then stand in front of a mirror reciting these mispronunciations. This will destroy your false identification with your ego.

Enter the mind of Edgar Dégas, the French artist. Try to peel an orange the way Dégas would.

Angels disguise themselves, like spies. In fact, angels *are* spies reporting to Heaven.

A house without inhabitants begins to decay, like a corpse.

Should you learn 136 words in one language or one word in 136 languages?

    It's up to you.

Monks throw the worst parties.

Follow a sport no one else has ever heard of. That way you'll avoid ugly arguments.

The next time you buy an umbrella, choose one that will cause general dismay.

Even if you're wealthy, live one day a month in extreme poverty.

A beach is a tiny desert near water.

Every language has numbers.

When you fall in love, don't fall completely in love. Let 10–12 percent of your mind remain skeptical.

We are all amateur doctors—some of us quite skilled, many of us quacks.

In a knife fight, always circle to the left.

You need not use a pumpkin to make a jack-o'-lantern. Almost any vegetable or large fruit will work. A watermelon makes a chilling Halloween head, with glowing red eyes. Try a jack-o'-lantern rutabaga! Or even a tiny, grinning radish.

If someone stops you as you're walking in Manhattan and asks you, "Which way to 34th Street?" tell them, "Ultimately, there's no reason to go to 34th Street."

If you're sent to Hell, don't complain. Satan hates whiners.

Anywhere you feel at home is your home. If you feel at home in Italy, Italy is your home. If you feel at home at your friend Larry's house, that is your home. A person can have forty thousand homes.

Sometimes cinnamon is a big mistake.

Parades are in decline. Americans are sick of standing in one place watching John Philip Sousa marches drift down a boulevard. See if you can design a more appealing parade: one with floats resembling giant rubber gloves, with people atop them dressed as periodontists tossing strawberries only to the ugliest people in the crowd. (Or perhaps an even better idea!)

Try to be kind to your neighbor, even if he dislikes you. Sometimes neighbors change their minds.

Try to use gossip as a force for good.

Fame expires, like a library card.

If you have a serious problem in your kitchen, call the Red Cross for help. Red Cross workers can be extremely helpful.

All animals dislike rock 'n' roll.

Great literature is full of erroneous mathematics.

Change your name every day, but don't tell anyone. Keep a diary with a list of your secret names.

Almost everything Facebook "knows" about you is wrong.

Remember, your body is composed of a vast number of cells, which work together in harmony. You are not one being; you are 37.2 trillion beings.

If you meet the Buddha on the road, ask him: "Which way to Pittsburgh?"

We are born naked and die in a hospital gown. In the course of our lives, we accumulate one article of clothing.

Give away all your money, but very slowly.

It is up to you to save our planet, because I certainly can't do it.

Too much religion, like too much sex, is debilitating.

"Envy parking" means driving through a parking lot yearning for all the good spots that are already taken.

Never reveal to a stranger the magazines you read.

A single chopstick is useful for eating molasses.

Masturbation should be done at home, or onstage with an electric guitar—nowhere else.

Remember, you can have more than one favorite color at a
time. And black is a color.

While you are asleep, just sleep. Don't play Scrabble or buy a
car. Concentrate on sleeping.

Distrust anything anyone tells you—except me. I can't harm
you. I'm a book.

Create your own distinctive sauce, giving it a title from literature. Here's one example:

Wuthering Heights Dip

> 1 oz. Riesling
> 1 raw egg
> sprig of rosemary
> pinch of salt

> Blend together. Serve on toast.

It's best to have two teddy bears so that when you're gone, they
can cuddle together.

Suppose your body were inside out: your spine on the outside,
your skin buried within. Would you still have friends?

Never kill an animal larger than your foot.

Children understand life better than grownups because they play tag.

If you must meet someone in a department store, rendezvous in the appliances section, next to the largest refrigerator.
This trick never fails.

We all worship the same God, but we each have a different demon.

If you are searching for meaning in your life, read the memoir of a lion tamer.*

*I recommend *Lioness of Judah: A Jewish Lion Tamer's Memoir* by Sarah Hauptman.

Many Americans have an irrational fear of punctuation— especially semicolons. Don't worry; they can't harm you.

Before you buy an air conditioner, make sure you like its hum.

One drinks to forget, but smokes ganja to remember.

Some people are *too* patient. They will wait an hour to be served in a restaurant, instead of waving to a waitress.

Stand close to a tree. Taste its oxygen.

A song without words is like a painting without shapes.

French fries are excellent for spelling words. The next time you eat French fries, spell out "Joy" or "Being" or "Love"—then eat the word.

Keep your mind large and your wardrobe small.

It's better to do good deeds cynically than to be a fervent idealist who does nothing.

No one ever sets out to tap their foot; they just do it unconsciously. But they're missing the pleasure of intentional tapping. Here's how to do it. Choose a delightful song, play it, and tap your foot—first your left, then your right. Continue alternating feet until the song ends.

[Note: Never tap both feet at the same time.]

You can mourn someone before they die. Choose a spot as your friend's "grave," erect a headstone (out of paper), sit beside it and weep.

Do you have a word you absolutely despise? You should. Open the dictionary and read until you find a word you hate. (For me, it's "nocent," which means "causing injury; harmful." Come to think of it, it's the opposite of "innocent.")

Falling in love is pleasurable, but falling out of love is even better. You weep, drink whiskey, walk the streets all night, wallow in self-pity. It's a pleasure for you, alone—you need not share it.

Here's a test to find out if you are psychic. Close your eyes and try to guess the next sentence in this book.

Buy a connect-the-dots book, but connect the wrong dots. Draw a line from number two to number thirteen, from number five to number eighteen. Construct awkward shapes!

Invent a legendary hero, such as Paraguma, a being who can transform any book into a movie.

Help people who want to be helped. If they refuse help, tell them, "I respect you for that."

Go to church until it sickens you. Then quit.

In your living room, take five steps forward. Then five steps back. Then five steps forward. Then five steps back. Continue for twenty-one minutes. This is known as a "conceptual treadmill."

Fifty percent of all money is wasted.

Try this recipe:

Inside-Out Sandwich

Shape peanut butter into the form of two slices of
bread. Bake at 375° for 32 minutes. Remove peanut
butter slats, and allow to cool. Place a slice of bread
between them, slathered on both sides with jelly.

God began as a Father, but gradually became a slightly dis-
tracted Aunt.

Instead of traveling, wake up one morning and pretend you're
in Holland.

Everyone needs either love or chocolate.

How many sculptors carve their own gravestones?

Buy a blank journal and write down all your wisdom. Then fill
the rest of the pages with doodles.

Death is an extravagance each of us can only afford once.

The gods know everything about you except your next move.

Clothing should have the same colors as fruit.

Every genius steals from previous geniuses.

Angels write on scrolls; demons send emails.

If you obey the law, you need never worry about your fingerprints.

When a poet says at a poetry reading, "I just have two more short poems," those poems are never short.

　　Here is a short poem:

New Way to Clean Your Room

　　Roll around on the floor.
　　Go outside.
　　Dust yourself off.

The point is not to believe in God but to force God to believe in you.

Baby billionaires have no idea they're wealthy.

If you are tall, enter a supermarket and search for a small person who needs help reaching a high item. Retrieve the item for them, then leave the store.

　　This is known as "height assistance."

Every sunrise is a refutation of night.

Ask twelve of your friends to follow you around for a week.
Find out what it's like to be Jesus.

Homework assignment: invent a new alphabet.

Practice "substitution cooking." Choose a recipe from a cookbook and substitute a different food for each ingredient. For
example, here is Steak-Potato Casserole from Myra Waldo's
The Casserole Cookbook:

> 1½ pounds potatoes, peeled and sliced thin
> 2½ teaspoons salt
> ¾ teaspoon freshly ground black pepper
> 1 cup chopped celery
> 2 cups thinly sliced onions
> 1 cup sliced green peppers
> 1½ pounds ground beef
> 1 20-ounce canned tomatoes, drained

Substitute rutabaga for the potatoes. Instead of salt,
use honey. Replace the pepper with cumin. Use rhu-
barb in place of celery. Instead of onions, add ginger.
Instead of green peppers, try snow peas. Replace
the beef with shrimp. Use sweet potatoes in place
of tomatoes. Rename the recipe: "Shrimp-Rutabaga
Casserole."

Every time you get a new idea, throw out one of your old ideas.

Freedom makes one happy; servitude makes one sluggish.

Thousands of numbers, all together, can add up to zero.

You can't stay in Little League forever.

Dogs are workaholics; cats are semi-retired.

Live your life as if you were made of turquoise.

Sing a duet with the next song that comes on the radio. Try to "out-sing" the singer.

No one buys a house at night.

Most problems can be solved by lying in bed for twelve minutes.

Amoebas are immortal. They don't die; they simply split in half. The first amoeba whoever lived is still alive in the form of billions of "descendants." That's why I wrote this poem:

Strange Fact

All amoebas have the same last name.

I heard a story, supposedly true, about an inmate in an upstate New York prison who was sent to solitary confinement. As he was being placed in his lonely cell, a guard—perhaps out of compassion—threw in a book of Buddhist scriptures.

When the prisoner walked out three months later, he was glowing.

Some of the advice in this book is deliberately awful, to discourage blind obedience.

I dreamed that my wife and I had a suicide pact. Violet went into the bedroom to kill herself, while I drank a dropper full of herbal tincture in the bathroom. I started to black out and ran into the bedroom shouting: "I don't want to die!"

It's usually a bad idea to commit suicide, even in a dream.

Find a Learning Partner. Stand with your partner and recite this vow:

> Everything you know, I will learn.
> Everything I know, you will learn.

Then shake hands, or hug, or touch each other in some way.

Stillness is a prerequisite for love.

Write yourself a letter occasionally. Stay in touch. Just as it's possible for two people in a marriage to drift apart, one person can drift away from herself.

Every third blessing is actually a curse.

Calculate the hypotenuse of your bedroom. Lay along that imaginary line. Breathe deeply.

Never drink a liquid that's fluorescent red.

PART 6

Extended Epiphanies

My Dream House

☀ ☀ ☀

I've been making notes on my Dream House. Here are some preliminary thoughts:

1) I am still, in my sixties, a graffiti artist. Don't tell the cops, but sometimes when I'm in New York City and no one's watching, I'll write: "Legalize counterfeit money!"—or some such inspiring adage—on a poster for Time Warner. I'd also like to decorate my own walls, but without inflicting permanent damage. The solution: an all-chalkboard room, with erasable surfaces instead of walls. Then I could emulate the character in Chuck Berry's brilliant "Memphis, Tennessee":

> *My uncle took the message and he wrote it on the wall.*

2) I don't know about your neighborhood, but where I live, at the foot of Romer Mountain in Phoenicia, New York, winds come pouring around, down the slope, quite often. If I could channel those gusts, I'd never have to sweep my house again! Two wind portals, one at each end of my doublewide trailer, would accomplish this pleasing task. "My cleaning lady is invisible," I could correctly remark.

3) I find the solidity of floors a little disconcerting. (Also, I have bunions.) It would be nice to provide a room with a water-floor: a room-sized waterbed, only two or three inches deep, which could massage one's feet while one dances to Max Powow's powerful new song, "Stay Busy":

> I stay busy; you stay busy;
> Busy as a garbageman on Monday!

4) It's the isolation of American life that most rankles me. In 1897, Manhattan installed a series of pneumatic tubes connecting office buildings so they could communicate with stunning speed. (These tubes functioned until 1953!) How much easier it would be to connect all the houses here on High Street! Anytime you wanted to talk to a neighbor, you could just shoot them a little high-speed note. (Yes, I've heard of email, but it lacks the physicality of a handwritten, folded-up page. Besides, with the High Street Pneumatic Tube one might send small quantities of sugar, salt, marijuana, postcards, etc.)

5) And wouldn't it be pleasant if people had movable houses that could connect like Lego pieces, allowing you to live communally for several days or weeks, until you got sick of each other? Imagine if our friends Clark and Perdita could just link their house to ours, and we could have chatty card games and dinners for the next six weeks!

6) I spend a lot of time in bed, daydreaming—so I could use three beds, in three bedrooms: one for thinking in English, one for French, one for Hebrew.

7) And while we're dreaming, why should our Dream House be an actual house? How much nicer to live in a large balloon, and to gaze out at the world through its translucent walls. (I would prefer yellow.) A balloon is waterproof, and, more importantly, round. Within its rubbery walls, one escapes the horrible rectangularity of modern living. And once you consume all the air within the house, you simply burst it with a pin, before you asphyxiate. Then you hook up the air pump to your next balloon-home!

8) Or a mushroom! Thanks to genetic engineering, scientists can easily create a fungus that grows thirty feet in diameter within a couple of days. Then you simply carve out an interior space—including doors and windows, even a table for your laptop—and move in! As with a balloon, you're liberated from the rectilinear, plus your home is an organic being. Once your dwelling decays, you move out, or grow another one!

The Perfect Wedding

❋ ❋ ❋

Recently a friend asked me: "If you could perform a wedding, what would it be like?" Well, in fact, I have performed three weddings in my life—all illegal. In two cases, the celebrants weren't looking for a "true" marriage; in the third instance, the couple was married by a Justice of the Peace before I arrived. But I didn't have complete control over these nuptials; the marrying couples designed the solemnities. What if I could create my own ceremony? Let me see …

1) How about an entirely nude wedding? (And I mean *entirely*: the bride, the groom, the bridesmaids, the groomsmen, the maid of honor—and of course, the clergyman!)

2) I would love to sing an entire wedding, as an oratorio. Admittedly, I tend to go off key, but I love singing, and a tone-deaf couple—with musically ignorant family and friends—would, I'm sure, be deeply moved.

3) A minimalist wedding, where I choose one word out of the Bible as the entire sermon. Let me do it right now, for practice:

Field.

[Full disclosure: I don't own a copy of the Bible, so I used the Koran.]

4) "Disneybounding" refers to Disney fans subtly "quoting" the style of their favorite characters, such as a pearl necklace or a hairdo, in order to evade the Disney World rules against adults dressing exactly like Disney cartoons. I'd love to perform a Disneybounding ceremony—especially if I could marry Olaf (the snowman from *Frozen*) to Donald Duck!

5) An elevator is a cozy—and cheap!—location in which to exchange vows. (For a large wedding party, a freight elevator is preferable.) How pleasant to rise upwards while entering the state of wedded bliss.

6) The Pope married a couple in midair! Here's what happened: Paula Ruiz and Carlos Elorriga, two Chilean flight attendants, wished to wed, but could not easily do so, because their church was destroyed in the 2010 Chilean earthquake. So Pope Frances himself performed their nuptials on Airbus 321, traveling from Santiago to Iquique, a city in northern Chile. This was the first Papal midair wedding in history.

Anything the Pope can do, I can do better! I am happy to marry hang gliders, parachutists, and astronauts in outer space. (Also, I would marry two space aliens—or even three!)

7) How about a wedding staged as a heavyweight boxing match, where the two "contenders" come out of opposite corners, dressed in striped shorts, wearing boxing gloves, and I stand in the center, in the garb of a referee? I might announce:

In this corner, weighing a hundred and sixty-five pounds, from Laguna Beach, California: "Jostling" Jeffrey Scott Gordinier! And in this corner, weighing a hundred and twenty-eight pounds, from Los Angeles, California: "Lucky" Lauren Elyse Fonda! I want to see a clean wedding, no hitting below the belt—and remember, protect yourself at all times!

8) Alexander Dumas said: "No one needs a poet until someone dies or gets married; then a poet is essential." It occurs to me that I am a poet, so perhaps I could read my poems in a wedding rite. For example:

No Reason to Love You

I have no reason to love you.
You're not that good-looking, or smart.
Your wardrobe is atrocious.

But I love you, uncontrollably,
ceaselessly.

I wish your teeth were nicer,
or you said something interesting.

But I love you, for no reason,
no reason at all.

Full of Love

I'm so full of love
I even love my dentist.
In fact, I love *your* dentist!

Love Poem

I was

an

"Army

of

One"

but

now

I'm a

Navy

of

Two.

9) But whatever type of wedding I officiate, I'll give this speech:

"If there is a God, may God bless every moment of your union. And if, as we all suspect, God is a myth, may every tree and shoe store and water fountain bless you. May blessings arise from each street corner and cell phone, and cover you as you walk.

"Everyone knows that marriage requires compromise, but the question is: 'Who should win each compromise?' (Because deep down, we all know one side always wins a compromise.) And the answer is: the wife should win. Maybe every nine hundred compromises, the guy should come out ahead. But in general, women deserve the upper hand. (One reason: women are usually right.)

"But, most of the time, forget which one of you is the 'man' and which is the 'woman.' These are outdated terms. A woman is just a man who shaves his legs. A man is just a woman who shaves her face. And stop shaving your face and legs! Concentrate on the important matters in life: playing card games and doing crossword puzzles. That's what marriage is for. Americans turn everything into work, which is why they are always exhausted.

"My advice is: just think to yourself, 'I'm getting married for the next twenty-five minutes.' Twenty-five minutes from now, decide if you want to renew this legal bond, or if you'd rather file for divorce. Twenty-five minutes later, decide again. Continue in this manner until you either die or fall in love with the furnace repairman.

"We have been misled by Hollywood films to believe that love must be between a young man and a young woman, bicycling together near a lake. But you can't bicycle forever, and there isn't always a nearby lake. In fact, there are forty-five thousand types of love, most of them invisible to us. Amoebas experience love; so do turnips. Two people standing in line together at the Motor Vehicles Bureau feel a subtle communion. Water falls to earth in the form of rain, or snow, or hailstones—out of love. Forget 'romance'! Open your eyes to all the loves surrounding you. In fact, you may love everyone you meet, as long as you don't sexually proposition them. Good luck!"

The Aroma of Home

☀ ☀ ☀

The term "home improvement" brings to mind hammers, ladders, jigsaws, and plywood. But I want to talk about air. In particular, the smells inhabiting the air. I'm not interested in Lysol, air fresheners, or even incense, or anything that requires spending money. I'm talking about the smell of dinner.

When a visitor walks in a house, she smells the place before she sees it. The smell of a tasty meal feels like a blessing in a home, just as the smell of burnt rice registers as a curse. (So be vigilant while cooking, lest your charred pinto beans send out malevolent nasal messages!) Oenophiles (wine-lovers) have developed a large vocabulary for describing the smell, which is called the "nose," of their favorite beverage: "appley," "raisiny," "cigar box," "floral," "oaky," "musty," "spicy." Similarly, one may speak of the "nose" of a household.

As I write, I am cooking a pot of curried butternut squash-tomatoes-cabbage-cilantro-green beans. Curry lends a pleasing 730 BCE flavor to a kitchen. (I've also added black pepper, fresh ginger, cayenne.) Because I follow a traditional yogic diet, I avoid onions and garlic, lending my cooking aroma a soft, baby-cheeks shape.

It's almost impossible to describe smells in language, but let me give it a try:

> Basil: sunlight on a stone bench
> Cumin: a deep cave in Egypt
> Sage: a thin waterfall
> Celery seed: an Iowa farmhouse
> Cardamom: a deserted beach in New Guinea
> Fenugreek: birch woods in July
> Ginger: a particularly slow-moving baseball game

The ancient Greek poets wore laurel wreaths as a crown of glory. Leaves from the bay laurel tree are still employed in cooking, so when you stir bay leaves into a soup, you're disseminating the smell of classical poetic headgear.

I hate waste, so I try to use every spice on my spice rack, some of which just appeared somehow (perhaps as gifts from friends moving to Istanbul?). Caraway seeds make an excellent addition to salad dressing, for example.

Have you ever noticed how cooking smells wend their way through a house like a sinuous cat? Two hours after I finish making dinner, I'll smell it in my bedroom, though the scent has vanished from the intervening three rooms.

Aroma nourishing requires no effort at all! You must cook anyway, and you wish your food to be appealing, so you add a variety of spices. I'm just asking you to observe how a succulent smell nourishes your dwelling. And how your friend Dan walks through the front door and tastes your soup with his nostrils.

The most seductive scent in a house is baking. I only occasionally make pastries, but my most recent offering, eggless applesauce cake (recipe from *The Spice and Spirit of Kosher-Jewish Cooking*) was moist and lightly brown—a solid success. Does everyone have a fruit-ripening basket? My wife and I do. At the moment, three cherry tomatoes and six avocados inhabit this enclosure. (I hate to be a botany nerd, but both avocados and tomatoes are technically fruits.) The tomatoes have a near-mint flavor when you sniff them close up; the avocados give off a solemn air of gestation.

And don't forget the satisfying olfactory benefits of brewing tea. Even normal orange pekoe is alluring, but "hippie" flavors like Demigod Nectar and Chocolate Frog create formidable force fields of smell.

Plants in a house oxygenate the air. Though oxygen theoretically has no smell, I suspect one internally recognizes its benefits to the scent-ecology. Currently, Violet and I have only an aloe plant—but it's a profuse one, resembling thirty-one interlacing snakes. Its smell is mild, curative, and green.

Another subtle influence on domestic atmosphere is candlelight. If you have rich relatives who insist on giving you gifts, ask for a beeswax candle. It's the best cent-for-scent investment.

My wife and I use all-natural cleansers, not to improve our house's "nose," but because we mildly fear chemicals. Still, there's a faint aroma of *Citrus grandis* (grapefruit) peel oil in our kitchen from Seventh Generation dishwashing liquid, and a trace of chamomile and lemon verbena from Nature's Gate shampoo in the bathroom. Violet also keeps a small arsenal of essential oils for bathing: eucalyptus, rosemary, lavender, tea tree oil. (For the record, my favorite essential oil is rosemary, with its faintly Nordic air of intrigue.) When I stay in a hotel,

I'm always appalled by the caustic cleansers and plastic-bouquet perfume in my room. An American hotel room is about as domestic as a carwash.

I need not enumerate the fetid smells that emerge from the human body—let alone the body of the dead mouse trapped in your pantry walls. Ironically, the same food that perfumes your house as it cooks emerges in a less appealing form from the rear of your torso the next day.

Just outside my stuffy Catskills house is the most remarkable deodorizer on Earth: the wind. Even in winter, try to open a window once a day to admit the purifying air. (And in summer, windows may remain open always, except during rainstorms.) I smell water in the wind on my road—a road that parallels Esopus Creek. Also, there's a hint of hemlock, pine, spruce. And wind works swiftly! Seven minutes with the window open utterly transforms a bedroom.

Time has passed, and I've now roasted the seeds from the butternut squash. (Remember that curry recipe from earlier?) The smell is succulent: somewhere in between turkey gravy and candy.

[Full disclosure: Unfortunately, I have received no payment for promoting Seventh Generation and Nature's Gate.]

My Father at One Hundred

Two weeks ago, my father turned one hundred. My sister organized a big party for him at the River Cafe in Brooklyn, a swanky restaurant right on the East River. I gave a speech in which I announced that Dad had been a member of the Communist Party. "If my father and his comrades have been successful and created a socialist revolution, I'm sure there would be much to criticize," I said. "But they failed, and I can only celebrate their legacy. American Communists fought for unions, to improve the lives of workers, and they struggled against murderous racism. Eventually, most of the members of the CPUSA left the party and had to reinvent themselves. Some of them, like Pete Seeger and my father, translated the Communist ideals into deeds of service and compassion. For some reason, such people have long lives. The gods are apparently pro-Communist."

My father, Jack Samuel Gorelick, was born in Scranton, Pennsylvania, in 1919. His parents were Russian Jews; together they ran Gorelick's Dress Shop in the working-class neighborhood of Pinebrook. My father was surrounded by anti-Semites as a child, and he jokes that he willed himself to grow tall. His parents were barely five feet tall; he grew to be six foot three.

Here, I am a little unclear about my father's chronology. He graduated from a technical high school, moved to New York City, and lived in the Jewish Lower East Side. He attended Columbia University, non-matriculated, where he met his best friend, Jimmy McCluskey. They considered enlisting in the Abraham Lincoln Brigade to fight in the Spanish Civil War, but instead traveled to Miami to write the Great American Novel. (They failed.)

My father returned home, attended the University of Scranton, received a bachelor's degree. He worked in a munitions plant in New Jersey, welding propellers for airplanes. (By then, our nation had entered World War II.) He joined the Navy and became a machinist mate first class, fixing airplane engines for the Naval Air Force. After the war, he was an organizer for the Union of Electrical Workers. My dad was revealed to be a Communist by the House Unamerican Activities Committee and was forced to leave the union.

He married my mother, moved to New York City, and worked in a machine shop, until he was blacklisted as a Communist. Then Dad began a career working with developmentally disabled adults and continued that occupation for the rest of his life, for another sixty-five years. On the way, he got a PhD in psychology from Yeshiva University.

For those of you who wish to live a hundred years, I asked my father his secrets.

"Optimism," was his first response. "My own father would say, 'Why complain? Is anything going to change if you complain?' My parents were great role models—and they were fairly long-lived." (My father has lived to one hundred partly to honor his own parents!)

"I very seldom get yelling-angry, because I don't think it does any good," my father told me. "What the hell is the point of it? You upset yourself, and you isolate yourself. If you yell at a person, nobody's going to say, 'Thanks. Thanks a lot.'"

He continued, "You know what I say: 'Never give up; never give in.'" For some people, everything is political. My father won't buckle under to death any more than he would buckle under to Joe McCarthy and the Red Scare in the 1950s.

"Be a people person." That's a third piece of advice from my dad. He went on to tell a story from Ernest Hemingway's *To Have and Have Not*. Harry Morgan, the gunrunner, is on his deathbed. "One man alone...," Harry says. A silence descends around the bed. Finally, Harry continues: "One man alone ain't got a bloody fucking chance."

This story has two morals: 1) Learn to rely on other people, and 2) don't be afraid to curse. Numerous obscene expletives keep my father young.

My father admitted that he has a terrible diet, but I pointed out that he eats the food he loves, like knishes and salami, and that he eats in moderation. In fact, Dad does everything in moderation. He asked his doctor how much alcohol he could safely drink in a day, and the answer was two fingers of scotch, so every night my father has exactly that much Johnnie Walker Black diluted with six ounces of seltzer. Even when my father smoked, he did so sparingly.

My father's mental faculties are perfectly fine, and perhaps he himself is responsible. He reads the *New York Times* every morning, and up until recently played three hours of chess a day on Yahoo. About twenty years ago, Dad taught himself to read Yiddish, which he still tries to do every day. Dad also does daily weight lifting exercises with soup cans.

Recently, my father started studying Russian. "I'm a great believer in: 'Use it or lose it,'" he said.

"I'm a psychologist; I know my IQ. I'm smart, but I'm not as smart as I thought I was. I have this notion: 'If you can do it, I can learn.'

"I'm patient. I'm pretty patient," Dad said.

I've learned from my father to make small progress, day by day, whether it's reading Chekhov or studying French. You wake up each day because the book you're reading is calling to you.

Recently my father was watching Laurence Olivier in *Hamlet*, the movie from 1948. Dad made two comments. One was: "Hamlet is older than his mother." (In those days, a movie studio would cast Olivier as Hamlet even though he was forty-one.) The other was: "I want to see how it's going to turn out." He said this when I went to sleep at two in the morning and he was still watching. Maybe that's how you make it to a hundred, by being always curious about how the movie's going to turn out.

"You know, you may live to a hundred and twenty; you better prepare yourself!" my father warned me.

Lincoln's Lost Speech

※ ※ ※

Abraham Lincoln's "Lost Speech" was delivered on May 29, 1856, in Bloomington, Illinois. Tradition states that the text was lost because Lincoln's powerful oration mesmerized every person in attendance. Reporters laid down their pencils, forgetting to take notes. In 2006 a fragment of the Lost Speech was found in the archives of a Baptist church in Bloomington. Through a distant cousin, I obtained it:

> A monarch provides security; it is comforting to bow to a Sire. But our nation was born of another wish. We are all part-kings here. If you bow to one man, you must bow to all.

Two Women Speak to Me About Crossword Puzzles

Here is a journal entry of mine from 2016:

> At an art opening in Catskill, I meet two women
> in their sixties, who tell me stories about the *New
> York Times* crossword puzzle. "My first husband and
> I used to do the crossword puzzle together," the
> shorter woman says. "We'd meet twice a week to do
> it."
>
> "You mean, after you were divorced?"
>
> "Yes. We'd meet on Friday to do the Friday puzzle,
> then we'd meet on Sunday to do the Saturday puzzle.
> And we were also still … involved. Even though he'd
> remarried! And his wife never left him."
>
> He was Irish, she Armenian. They met when she
> was seventeen and he was twenty-one. Now he's
> been dead for three years. She lives on 60th Street in
> Manhattan.
>
> Meanwhile, the other woman, Simone Feldstein,

reads the *New York Times* cover to cover every day. "Do you do the crossword puzzle?" I ask.

"Are you kidding? In all the years I've been reading the *Times*, I've gotten maybe one word. But back when I was looking to meet guys, I would go to a bar and do the crossword puzzle in ink. I wouldn't put down the right answers, just any word that came to mind."

"And did it work?" I ask.

"Oh, yeah! You'd be surprised how many guys I got that way. Sometimes they'd say to me, 'Let's do the puzzle together.' And I would answer, 'No, I must work on it alone!'"

If you are looking for a companion in life, you might wish to consider Simone's strategy.

Thieves

I attempt to live a morally unblemished life, but I have one vice: I steal toothpaste. If I'm staying at someone's house and I see, in the bathroom, say, a tube of Tom's Strawberry Toothpaste for Kids, I'll place some on my toothbrush and try it. My main motivation is curiosity.

Let me explain. Often, I'll ask permission, but sometimes it's too early, or too late. I don't want to burst in while a mother is feeding her two kids, or a couple is making love, to ask: "Do you mind if I filch a minuscule amount of your dentifrice?"

Nonetheless, theft is theft. Philosophically, it's the same to steal .06 ounces of toothpaste as it is to steal a Maserati. I write this essay, in part, to apologize to my past and future victims.

Especially my latest ones: three people in a housing complex in Berkeley whom I didn't really know. They were friends of my friend Mica. Ironically, the name of the toothpaste was "Thieves." Its subtitle was: "A Natural Toothpaste Fortified with the Germ Fighting Ingredients Thymol and Eugenol." It tasted very Californian: herbal and clean.

If you are searching for a vice that is not terribly destructive, I suggest toothpaste theft. (Though, for obvious reasons, this vice should not be practiced during pandemics.)

PART 7

Eat Your Dreams, the Ultimate Diet

A DISCOVERY

I am on a new regime—attempting to eat less in the evenings, so I will lose weight. Thus, I go to sleep hungry. Two nights ago, I had a dream. I was standing in my old apartment in the East Village of Manhattan, which I left seven years ago. A bowl of sesame noodles sat on the table. I began to eat the noodles—without sitting down. They were excellent.

I woke up no longer hungry.

The next day I told this story to my wife, and while speaking to her I realized: I have discovered the perfect diet! You may feast on any food, and never gain weight. The secret is to eat in your dreams.

THE VALUE OF DREAMS

Of course, in order to benefit from feasting in your dreams, you must remember them. "How do I do that?" you ask. The first step is simple: consider your dreams worthy.

In this culture, dreams are not valued. Why? Because they are, supposedly, not "real." But who is to say what is "real"?

Consider movies. You spend fifteen dollars (in New York City) to sit in a dark room for two hours. When you emerge, what do you have to show for it? Nothing. (Unless, for some reason, you hold onto your popcorn container.) You don't even receive a program. Yet you consider this experience "real."

Meanwhile, when you lie in a dark room and watch movies

for five hours—movies which star *yourself* (at night), you consider these meaningless.

The soft-rock band Bread sang, in 1971,

> Dreams are for those who sleep;
> Life is for us to keep

in "I Want to Make It with You." This lyric expresses the typical anti-dreaming sentiment of our culture.

I say: "Defy Bread! Admit that you are one of 'those who sleep'! There is no shame in sleeping, nor in the nectareous romance of dreams!"

HOW TO REMEMBER YOUR DREAMS

Remember, dreams are shy. Like visitors who easily feel unwanted, they will quickly find an excuse to leave. You must let your dreams know you appreciate them.

One easy way is to have a "dream-friend." This is someone you write (or tell) your dreams to every day—or as often as you recall them. It's like a "tennis buddy." This kind of writing is perfect for email, but you may also use postcards, or velvet-edged stationery.

A dream-friend is not always easy to find. You must test out your acquaintances, to learn who is dream-sympathetic. You may be surprised. Your friend Edna, the potter, may despise dreams, while Frank, the investment banker, might have a juicy, layered dream life.

QUIT YOUR JOB

Work is the enemy of dreams. When you wake up and rush to work, your dreams quickly vanish. One easy solution to this dilemma is to abandon your job.

Simply walk into your boss's office (you need not knock) and say: "Ms. Fenlap (or Mr. Fenlap), I must announce my resignation! I need more time in the morning to recollect my dreams."

If your boss seems sympathetic, you may explain that you are following a groundbreaking new diet.

WAKE UP EARLIER

Another option is simply to wake up earlier. Give yourself an hour in the morning to cultivate dream recollections.

One advantage of this plan is that you will still earn money from your job.

A DREAM WALL

For some people, the best way to remember dreams is on a Dream Wall. Choose one wall of your house on which to transcribe your dreams. (Use colored pens!) You may also wish to draw salient images. The task-oriented will enjoy "filling up the wall"—and watching a mural of their Night Tales emerge.

DREAM MAPS

Another dream-mnemonic uses maps. Each morning when you awaken, open your Dream Atlas and circle the city or town where your dream took place. (You may also use colored dots.) On a separate sheet, note the date of the dream.

If you find that you dream often of a particular city—Berlin, for example—buy a map of that locality, to track your dream settings, street by street.

If you travel in dreams, you may indicate motion by a series of dashes on the map.

Often in mid-dream we don't know exactly where we are. Dream maps encourage you to notice your locations while dreaming. Eventually, you will look for street signs, rivers, landmarks, and other cues.

PAID-FOR DREAMING

One problem is that in our culture value is expressed through money. Dwayne ("The Rock") Johnson receives $23.5 million for a movie; therefore, he is successful. A fiddler receives $14 for a performance; thus, he is unimportant.

Dreams are unpaid. For this reason, we assume they are worthless.

There is a simple solution to this misperception. Send $100* to a close friend (or your mother). Arrange that each time you successfully remember a dream, your friend will mail you a five-dollar bill. Though this is a small sum—and ultimately your own money—psychologically, it will convince you that dreams are valuable.

*Of course, if you are rich, you can send $100,000 to your friend, and receive $5,000 for each dream.

A DREAM CLUB

Another way to remember dreams is to begin a dream club. Invite a number of acquaintances to gather every two weeks and recount their dreams. Each will begin a dream journal—plus, perhaps, a dream sketchbook—and will take turns reading.

In a more advanced dream club, you may choose certain dreams to act out, as performances.

Here is an interesting project for your Dream Club: give the assignment to write a fake dream. At the next class, read both real and counterfeit dreams. See if you can guess which is which!

For example, below are two dreams: one true and one false. Can you distinguish them?

> I must catch a plane to Paris. I am already late, and now I await a subway to take me to the airport (perhaps in New York City?). A large number of people lounge on the platform.
>
> A subway pulls into the station. I run toward the open doors and realize—I have no shoes! I took off my shoes while sitting, and forgot them.
>
> Looking down at a shelf below the platform, I see numerous shoes, and boots, in rows. Should I reach down and grab a pair of boots? What if they don't fit? And isn't that stealing, besides? And what about *my* shoes? Should I abandon them forever?
>
> I awaken.

I am in the Crusades, fighting in an army of
Christians just north of Jerusalem. I wear an iron
visor and chainmail, and carry a halberd.* A large,
angry Turkish man lunges at me. I duck, then strike
him.

Suddenly someone calls out: "Break!"

It is 3:00 p.m., time for our break. My enemy and
I stop fighting, and sit down to tea.

*A weapon with an axe-like blade and a steel spike.

BED CARE

A bed is a shrine to the Unconscious. Like a sailboat, it can
propel you to Madagascar—on the wings of sleep. If you take
special care of your bed, your bed will reward you with memorable dreams.

When you make your bed, bow or kneel reverently. Offer
your bed helpful support, or prayers.

Once or twice a day, walk into your bedroom and thank
your bed.

Notice if this improves your dreams.

SLEEPING ON COOKBOOKS

"How can I arrange for food to appear in my dreams?" I hear
you next ask.

One simple answer is to sleep on a cookbook. Place a collection of recipes under your pillow, before you don your paja-
mas. Quite possibly, the entrées will seep into your dreams.

Begin with basic cookbooks with which you are familiar, and move on to more exotic fare, such as *Victorian Picnic Salads*.

If, one Thursday, you are in the mood for Mexican food, lay *Viva Mexico!* by Salvador Escumar under your pillow. If there is a particular food you'd like—for example, barbacoa tacos—place a bookmark at that page.

Remember to be adventurous while dreaming. Try new foods! Dishes you may not enjoy in real life can taste wonderful in sleep.

If cookbooks don't work, try takeout menus, or even business cards from restaurants.

Another method is to simply write the name of the food you wish for on a slip of paper, and place it beneath your head. Or if you are more visually inclined, draw a picture—or cut out a photograph of the dish from *Family Circle* magazine, or *Gourmet*.

Warning: You may not always receive the food you want, in your dream life. Despite sleeping on top of *Szechuan Holiday*, you may find yourself eating spaghetti with olives. Dream-eating is not an exact science (at least not yet!).

SNIFFING

Here is another method to induce food-dreams: before you retire at night, sniff several culinary herbs. This may stimulate the Inner Cook.

At the end of the Jewish Sabbath, a ceremony called *Havdalah* is performed. Because the Jewish day begins at night, the ceremony also takes place at night—once three stars are visible. This ritual bids farewell to the Sabbath. In Havdalah, a spice box (called a *b'samim*) is passed around, symbolizing the departing sweetness of the Day of Rest. Commonly, the spice box contains cloves, cinnamon, or bay leaves.

Just as the scent of herbs consoles us over the loss of the Sabbath, your nightly herb-sniffing may evoke plentiful comestible dreams.

ANOTHER METHOD: A SETTING

For some, the best way to induce meal-dreams is to lay out a dinner setting, next to their bed. On a tray or small table, place a plate, fork, knife, spoon, and napkin in the proper positions. (If you don't know the exact positions, see *The Etiquette of Dining* by Gail A. Florence.) If you have the habit of blessing a meal, you may perform your benediction. (For some reason, it is extremely unusual to pray in a dream.)

Of course, you may vary the classical dinner setting. You may include six forks, or chopsticks. You may wish to embroider a cloth napkin: your "dream-napkin." On it, you may sew an image of the Dream Goddess, who grants you food dreams.

RENOUNCING FOODS

Soon after I became a vegetarian, I began to dream about eating meat. I would almost always eat chicken, usually fried. This forbidden food was succulent, almost erotic. Sometimes within the dream, I would rationalize to myself, "Although I shouldn't eat chicken, this is okay because it's a dream."

This suggests a strategy for meal-dreams. Simply give up a food—especially one you enjoy immensely—and wait. Within a month, I suspect, you will be devouring the proscribed dish in your sleep.

SHOPPING

Last night I visited a natural food store, in my dream. I was shopping for nuts, but I never bought any. I stopped to write in a notebook. (I am one of the few people who writes in dreams.) Then I awoke.

This natural food store was on the second floor, above another store. The space was small, and I stood near several open crockery pots containing cashews and almonds. I ate nothing, but I woke up without hunger—and I had fasted the day before!

Apparently merely food-shopping in dreams is enough to curtail hunger.

FASTING

Which brings me to my next thought: fasting. I fast every week, from Thursday at 6:00 p.m. to Friday at 6:00 p.m. I have been following this practice since 1975. Fasting becomes easy, if one pursues it regularly, I have found. Your body begins to think forward to the next fast.

Nonetheless, I cannot recommend fasting to you, the reader, legally. You must choose, with the aid of trusted medical supervisors, on your own.

But if you do fast, it seems likelier that you will eat in your subsequent dream!

PIZZA

Last night I dreamed I was in a convenience store. At one counter stood a woman who had just baked a large number of small pizza pies. They were laid out on the counter, which was reddish orange.

Each pizza was covered with a little layer of crumbs. The crumbs resembled ground nuts at first, but when I looked closely they seemed to be a spice.

"Is that oregano?" I asked the woman.

"Yes," she replied.

Then she told me that her boss had just called and canceled all pizza baking. These were the last pizzas she would ever prepare. She was distraught.

As we spoke, I began to eat one of the pizzas. It was not particularly tasty—doughy and generic. I couldn't taste the oregano. Again, I ate standing.

(But she didn't charge me. Not only was this food free, as all food in dreams is—this food was free *even in the dream*!)

OUR SLOGAN

Here is our slogan (the slogan of the Dream-Eating Movement):

"A hungry mind makes tasty dreams."

There is a long tradition that overeating before sleep can lead to distressing dreams. (Many early comic strips utilized this plot.) But the inverse has never been stated—skipping a meal makes lovely dreams. This is the first book to propose this logical thesis. Another slogan:

"Undereat—you'll be grateful tonight!"

BON MARCHÉ

Dreams are—as we say in French—*bon marché* [inexpensive].
In fact, dreams are cheaper than inexpensive—they are *gratuit*
[free].

It is quite possible to spend $14,000 on a meal. For example,
if you travel by private jet to the finest restaurant in Thailand—
which is *not* in Bangkok, but in the village of Nakhui, twenty
miles away—and order the best dish on the menu (Quo Hok
Trai), then spend the night in a suite of the premier hotel, the
Imperial Grove, you will easily spend this sum.

And yet, the same experience—perhaps even more lavish,
in fact—may be dreamed for the price of $0.

WHY I EAT STANDING UP IN MY DREAMS

Dreams are always hurried. (At least mine are.) For example, last night my daughter and I were trying to enter the
Metropolitan Museum (in my dream). Somehow, we reached
a high ledge above the entrance. Should we attempt to climb
down? I feared the drop was too far—that we would break our
legs if we leaped down.

But I couldn't see beyond the ledge—to see how far we
would fall.

Sylvia and I paced along the ledge. We were constantly
moving, seeking a way into the museum. We were *rushing*!

This is my point. Dreams are always propelled forward. So
occupied were Sylvia and I, we never thought to turn around
and go back the way we had come.

Eventually, vexed, I awoke.

This is why in two of my three eating dreams in this book, so far, I am standing.

WHAT IS FOOD?

When I was a boy, people ate out of duty. Science had decreed that certain foods—frozen lima beans boiled in a pot, carrot sticks—contained the vital elements necessary for life. Solemnly, one imbibed these useful nutrients while gathered with one's family around a table.

Today, we eat for pleasure. Food must be enjoyable—or more than enjoyable: explosively fun! We eat at our desk at the office, or in front of a thin-screen TV. Perhaps we watch our favorite show—*Dancing with the Stars*—while munching Doritos Collisions Chicken Sizzler Zesty Salsa Chips.* We cannot imagine purposefully eating boring food.

But what is enjoyment?

Enjoyment is a mental reflex, an interior condition of the mind. Food-happiness is not found within the molecules of potato chips. It is found within the self.

One day, you eat shrimp Lo Mein and are almost furious with delight. Two days later, you order it again and it tastes opaque, oily. What's the difference? It's the same dish from the same restaurant. The difference is in your mind (specifically the food-happiness plexus of the mind).

If the mind gives us pleasure—not the actual material food—it is fruitless to search for happiness in corn chips (or any other meal).

*Believe it or not, this is an actual Doritos flavor.

THE CONSERVATION OF PLEASURE

Luckily, there is Sparrow's Law of Conservation of Pleasure. It is based on the Third Law of Thermodynamics: Energy cannot be created or destroyed. The same, I claim, holds true for pleasure.

You are destined to have a certain amount of enjoyment each day. You may use it all up during the day, or you may avoid many pleasures, and savor them after sundown in your dreams.

All the delectable foods you refuse to swallow during daylight will await you, never fear! You will have every gustatory satisfaction, and still be thin.

YET ANOTHER METHOD

Last night I had a strange dream. My wife and I were walking up and down Dyckman Street in Manhattan, the street I grew up on. We were picking up large piles of dog poop. (Apparently, we had a dog in the dream who had deposited these piles earlier.) The piles were chunky and yellow.

As we walked, we argued. "No, that's not from *our* dog!" Violet shouted as I lifted one pile. She had that annoyed, how-can-you-be-so-stupid air that one has in an argument.

I woke without hunger.

(So apparently, this is another possibility. Dreaming about shit also allays hunger.)

DREAM RECIPE JOURNAL

After you awaken from an eating-dream, lie in bed as long as possible, trying to remember the shape, texture, and savor of your dream food. Particularly observe the subtle tastes, beneath the main taste. You will need this information to write your dream recipe journal.

Bring out your journal and try to recreate the preparation of the food. Write down each step, and each ingredient—even ones you are uncertain of.

Eventually, you will have an entire cookbook composed by your dream-mind.

A DINNER PARTY

On a full moon, invite friends over for a "dream meal." If possible, invite the people you ate with in your dreams. If not, invite those who are sympathetic to dreaming.

Cook several dishes from your Dream Recipe Journal. Serve to the guests.

Before the meal, say this grace: "We thank You, Goddess of Dreams, for sending us this food, through Your ephemeral, secretive stories."

ORANGES

Last night, in my dream, I bought a new car: a red roofless vehicle, almost like a jeep. In it, my friends and I traveled east from California across America. In Denver, we met a nice woman named Mary who threw us a small party at which she served only fruit. I remember oranges and nectarines. My friends were somewhat confused by this selection of food. They were sophisticated people, accustomed to more formal meals.

My own orange, unfortunately, was rather dry—the kind that, when peeled, breaks out in spiky shards.

I felt immediately close to Mary, however, and wrote her name on a small piece of paper so I wouldn't forget her. But when I awoke, the paper had vanished, and I can no longer recall her last name. (Something like "Thomas.")

ADVANCED CULINARY DREAMING

In advanced dreaming, one creates a sequence of related dreams. In the case of food-dreams, this may prove very useful. One night, you may prepare a dish—say, calamari salad—and the next night improve it, with a subtle puree of beet greens. Or you can wildly experiment: Try pasta embedded in carrots, for example. You may serve the same dish to different friends—or even to President Emmanuel Macron of France—on different nights.

Using advanced dreaming, one will easily become a brilliant chef (at least in the Nighttime World).

DONUTS

Last night I dreamed I was at a large banquet in a friend's house. Two rooms had been connected by opening a pair of double doors. A long, rough wooden table—like at an old English inn—had been erected. The hostess pointed to a basket of donuts beneath the table: "Take as many of these as you want! They're left over from this afternoon!"

They were smallish donuts, covered with a deep brown frosting—almost black. This frosting was thick, moist, and dripping. Though I didn't eat any, just looking at them was filling.

Some dream food may be savored with the eyes.

CHICKEN SOUP

In last night's dream I was sitting at a table, eating with friends. There was a long conversation, and I can't remember the topic. Was it the history of Russia? Were we doing a crossword puzzle together? Had my house burned down, and was I discussing that?

But I remember the soup clearly. I knew it was from a can. Probably it was Campbell's. The broth was thin—thinner than real Campbell's soup. There were vegetables, tiny segments of celery. I suspected that there was chicken, but I wasn't worrying about it.

Finally, at the end of the dream, which was also the end of the soup, I saw several fragments of chicken floating in my bowl. I could no longer deny I was eating chicken soup. Horror filled me—I was no longer a vegetarian!

But as I awoke, I realized this was a dream, that only a dream chicken had died to satisfy my hunger.

As I was washing my hands in the bathroom, I realized what I had experienced was truly Chicken Soup for the Soul.

FOOD IN BOOKS

For the last three years, I have been reading books in French. Soon after I moved to Phoenicia, I began to find French books on the free table of the Formerly Yours Thrift Shop. Since I had studied French for six and a half years in my youth, I could understand some of the words. A French-English dictionary helped with the rest. Now every week, I study with a Swiss woman named Claude, in Kingston. One of the books I am currently reading is *Le Spleen de Paris* by Charles Baudelaire. This book is a series of small sketches about life in France, published in 1869.

Recently, one story, "La Belle Dorothée" ["The Beautiful Dorothy"] has obsessed me. The story takes place in an unnamed village under the heat of a brilliant sun. "Le monde stupéfié s'affaise lâchement et fait la sieste..." ["The stupefied world sags languidly and takes a siesta."] Only one person is moving in the town: Dorothy, who walks "balançant mollement son torse si mince sur ses hanches si larges" ["voluptuously balancing her so-thin torso on her so-wide hips"]. Baudelaire continues:

> Why has she left her little hut, which is so charmingly decorated, where flowers and mats make a perfect boudoir (at so little cost), where she takes such pleasure in combing her hair, smoking, fanning herself, or gazing in the mirror at her feathered fans, while the sea, which breaks on the beach three hundred feet away, offers her unformed reveries a powerful and monotonous music, and the iron cookpot, where a ragout of crabs in saffron rice stews, sends her, from the back of the courtyard, its tantalizing scent?

That crab ragout has obsessed me—suddenly today I realized why. The food described in fiction is similar to the food found in dreams. You eat it with your mind, not your mouth.

DRINK YOUR DREAMS

This morning I was lying in bed and the phrase "drink your dreams" entered my mind. *What can this mean*, I pondered.

Then I realized that this book has far more implications than I originally imagined. Alcoholics can cure themselves by simply choosing to drink while dreaming. They need to abstain from alcohol only sixteen hours a day, while the other eight hours can be an intoxicating spree! Similarly, gamblers may stop betting by day, and visit the swankiest casinos at Monte Carlo at night—and win! Drug abusers, criminals, anyone with a compelling vice may abstain by daylight and wildly overindulge in bed, with their eyes closed.

Drink your dreams! Gamble your dreams! Snort your dreams!

THE GUN

Last night, in my dream, I visited a first-class restaurant. I dined alone, paid the bill, and left. A few hours later, I noticed my gun was missing. I must have left it at the restaurant, I decided. (But I was afraid to go back and ask: "Have you found my gun"?)*

Does this *mean* something? (For example, is it saying: "In order to eat, one must lay down one's gun"?)

(I don't remember the meal.)

*In real life, I am unarmed.

SLEEP FOOD MUSEUM

I recommend that you start a Sleep Food Museum in which to store treasures from your dream meals. This museum will exist only in the dreamworld. When you finish a dream you like, simply grab something from the dream, run over to the Sleep Food Museum, and display it there. For example, you may save: a fork from a restaurant, a menu, a bowl, the waiter's beard,* the maitre d's uniform.** Remember, space is not a problem in dream reality, so if you enjoy a particular restaurant, take the whole table with you for your Sleep Food Museum— or even the entire dining room!

And don't forget foods you prepare yourself in your dreams. Collect whisks, blenders, tongs, rolling pins.

And food itself! You need not worry about cockroaches, rats, or mold. Place an entire pound cake on display if you choose! It won't spoil!

*Simply cut it off!
**Ask the maitre d' to disrobe for you. And if he refuses, strip him!

HEROIN

Last night I dreamed I was in a house of prostitution (or more precisely, a cottage of prostitution—this was a rural brothel). I was alone, doing chores around the house.

I don't know how I got there—honestly! Probably, I was traveling and a kind woman allowed me to stay. Now I was "paying" for my lodging by helping out. (Often, I am indigent in my dreams.)

Someone had asked me to prepare her heroin; I was mixing it up. The drug was brown, not white, which surprised me. In my dream, as in life, I know nothing about the proper combination of heroin and water. The mixture came out lumpy, like poorly-made pancake batter.

I worried that the woman injecting it would overdose and die from my awkward preparation.

(I mention this dream because it's so much like cooking.)

YOUR DREAM GENEALOGY

You are not the first dreamer in your family. Generations have dreamed before you. In order to remember your dreams, you may wish to compile a dream genealogy.

Here's how it works. Ask your mother and father if they remember any dreams. Carefully transcribe everything they say. If your grandparents are alive, ask them the same question. If they are deceased, ask your parents if they recall their own parents' dream tales. Carefully research any written records of your ancestors. Extend your search to all the branches of your family.

Eventually you may create a family tree using key words to designate major dreams. For an example, see below:

halibut
cowboy
underwater helicopter
Boston
walrus in the bathroom
white gloves
big clock

shepherd's crook

trumpet

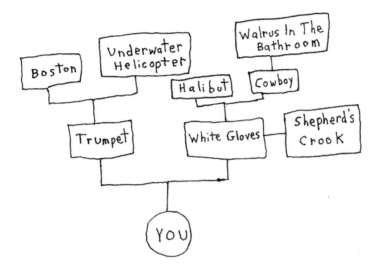

THE ABOLITION OF WAR

Have you ever murdered someone in your dreams? If so, you'll remember the admixture of emotions the moment you awoke: shock, self-loathing, and relief.

That dark-haired man you killed is still alive, you realize, with sudden happiness. (Though you still see him, bleeding face down on the floor, in dream memory.) In fact, you may even discover (as you awaken more fully) that he never lived at all!

You have harmed no actual living man. Your conscience is pristine. Yet you have experienced the grimy, complex terror of murder.

Every day, throughout the planet, men (and many women) join armies, touched by the thrilling promise of war. Unfortunately, they will often suffer and cause other creatures—even dogs and cats—to weep and lose their legs. If they could dream war, this would be unnecessary. Every night, they could fight large troops of soldiers—and win!

Dreams would replace warfare! Peace would come to humankind.

THE GOLDEN PEAR

In a dream last night, I was practicing my magical powers. I walked up to a row of fruits (which happened to be floating in the air) and tried turning them into gold. I touched the fruits—there were six or seven of them—*willing* them to transform.

Finally, after several attempts, they did; then I remembered: "Damn, I wanted to eat that pear! It was perfectly ripe!"

(Apparently, I did not know the "spell" for returning fruits to their original form.)

DREAM NOURISHMENT

The food we eat by day builds our bodies. The food we eat at night builds our dream-bodies. Both bodies are valuable. Our day-bodies allow us to live, work, converse. Our dream-bodies enable us to visit old friends—some of whom are dead—and to travel through the world (and to other worlds)!

Our dream-bodies seem to require very little food. We only eat in dreams once every few months. Dream food must be much more nourishing than earthly food. (Certainly, it is often vividly colorful.)

So don't delay! Throw out all your other diet books, and start eating your dreams! (But wash your hands thoroughly first, especially if you're in the midst of a pandemic!)

Acknowledgments

I must thank Violet Snow, my wife, for her supernal generosity, perceptiveness, and prayer. Marcus Boon, Charles Paikert, Dan Sofaer, Davida Luminabes, Alan Fliegel, David Congdon, Steve Kronen, and Caren Gould have always had faith in my shadowy "talent." Francine Vidal has been a stellar French tutor. Thank you to Paul Smart, Will Dendis, and Geddy Sveikauskas at Ulster Publishing, who gave me complete freedom—too much freedom—to compose instructional essays. Sy Safransky, editor of *The Sun* magazine, believed in me back when no one else would even give me a seat on the bus. At Monkfish Book Publishing Company, my editor, Susan Piperato, and my publisher, Paul Cohen, gently and genteelly willed this book into existence. If I had a literary agent, I'd thank her too.

About the Author

Sparrow lives in a doublewide trailer in Phoenicia, N.Y., with his wife Violet Snow. He has been published in *The New Yorker*, *The Sun*, *American Poetry Review*, *Chronogram*, and Ulster Publishing's newspapers, and he was once quoted in *Vogue*. He is the author of eight books of poetry and prose, regularly runs for president, and plays flutophone in the voluptuary pop group Foamola.